Starting the Dream!

How to Avoid a Nightmare When You Start a Business!

CHRIS BEKS

Published by Chris Beks 2023
Copyright © 2023 Chris Beks
www.ceebeks.com

All rights reserved. No part of this publication may be reproduced, stored in a retrieval
system, or transmitted in any form or by any means, electronic, mechanical, photocopying,
recording or otherwise, without the prior written permission from the publisher.

ISBN: 978-0-6484082-4-6

Disclaimer
Every effort has been made to ensure that this book is free from error or omissions.
Information provided is of general nature only and should not be considered legal or financial advice. The intent is to offer a variety of information to the reader. However, the author, publisher, editor or their agents or representatives shall not accept responsibility for any loss or inconvenience caused to a person or organisation relying on this information.

A catalogue record for this book is available from the National Library of Australia.

Book cover design and formatting services by Rasika Um, shashika.info

Endorsements

"With 60% of businesses set to fail after three years and 70% after a decade, this book will be an invaluable tool to any entrepreneur who wants to dive in and start their own business or for any business owner that needs some guidance. Having been in business for over 21 years myself, I have learned that you always need to be ahead of the curve and bring on board great experts to help you along the way to succeed.

Chris Beks is not only an outstanding expert when it comes to all things finance and accounting he has been a shining beacon for decades to many Australian companies who are looking for guidance."

Adrian Falk,
Founder Believe Advertising & PR

If you're starting a new business or are soon to do so, then you're in luck.

Chris Beks' "Starting the Dream" is the perfect read for you at just the right time. I only wish this book was around when I started my own business a decade ago!

You'll enjoy a ton of hard data to separate the romantic notions from the facts and guide you on your way to living your dream and avoiding a business-fuelled nightmare.

Highly recommended.

Angus Pryor
Multi-award-winning Marketing Agency Founder,
International speaker & Bestselling Author

"Chris Beks' book "Starting The Dream" is a must read for all new business owners.

Chris does an excellent job of going through all of the issues that you don't know you're about to face in business.

He also provides excellent advice on how to avoid these problems from occurring, and what to do should they occur.

Highly recommended!

Daimien Patterson
CEO
Integrityx Group of Companies

"When I started my business 21 years ago my dad who was an accountant warned me that 50% of businesses fail in the first 2 years.

This book is a must read for anyone starting a business who doesn't want to become a statistic."

Debbie O'Connor
Brand Strategist, Author and Presenter
White River Design & Brand Magic

"If you are considering starting your own business, then you need this book!

From years of experience and wisdom, Chris breaks down the challenges all new business owners face and simplifies the bests steps forward.

Reading like a 'How to Guide', the lessons within this book will set you up for success as your business grows.

Don't make the same mistakes others before you have.

Read, listen, learn, and take massive action!"

Ryan Goodwin
CEO of Mode Group, Multi Award Winning Entrepreneur

"Starting the Dream" is an easy to read, go-to guide bursting with advice and relatable stories.

Chris shares his vast knowledge and experience - from mastering the financials to looking after yourself - so you can avoid the pitfalls along the way to building your business successfully.

Helping you avoid the common problems on your journey to not just surviving but thriving in the world of small business."

Cindy Mitchell
Founder & Director, AquaDash Swim Gear

"Being in business for the past 35 years I thought I knew it all. The mistake I made that everything in business was in my head was the worst thing I could ponder."

"Chris Beks' book, 'Starting the Dream', not only covers business but how to look inward and look after myself."

" 'Starting the Dream' is ideal for all business owners who know deep down what they want but struggle to know where to begin."

"Thank you for this Roadmap Chris."

Kimon Kalligas
Fresh Space

Starting the Dream! is a must-read for anyone looking to venture into entrepreneurship or seeking to enhance their existing business. Chris Beks' wealth of experience shines through, making the book a reliable and informative guide.

I highly recommend it to all aspiring entrepreneurs as it provides the necessary knowledge and tools to navigate the complexities of the business world and avoid potential nightmares along the way.

The comprehensive roadmap for success laid out in the book is well-structured and easy to follow. The combination of expert insights and practical advice makes it a valuable resource for those serious about creating the perfect business, the one that is profitable, sustainable and provides freedom!

Stacey Hughes
Digital Marketer and creator of FAB ADS Academy

"Your dream will remain a dream if you don't put the right foundations in place, but this book is here to help you do that. Chris draws from years of personal experience as well as sharing up-to-date instructions for aspiring business owners who want to fast-track their success. A must-read!"

"This quick and easy read will put you light years ahead when it comes to starting and growing a business."

"Starting a business is harder than it looks but this book will save you from the missteps and pitfalls that lead to business owner dreams becoming nightmares."

"I really appreciated the clear information and steps in 'Starting the Dream', which is the perfect handbook for any aspiring business owner. It won't take you long to read it cover to cover, and the lessons can prevent so many setbacks. Don't start a business without reading this book!"

Clea Jones
Content Marketing Specialist

Contents

About Chris Beks	10
Preface	12
The Setting	14
The Characters	15
Plot	16
Foreword	18
Introduction	23
1. What the statistics tell us about business failures	24
2. Beginning: Why go into business?	26
3. Why running a business can be a nightmare	36
4. The Causes - what are the reasons why business fail?	44
1. Not seeking Professional Advice before starting	47
2. Financial instability - This can be described as a lack of proper financial planning and management and can lead to financial instability, which can cause a small business to fail	53
3. Lack of customers - A small business needs customers to survive. Without them, it will fail	58
4. Intense competition - Small businesses face ruthless competition from other businesses	85
5. Poor mindset - Poor management can lead to a lack of direction and a lack of control over the business	90

6. Unexpected legal or regulatory issues - Small businesses can be blindsided by unexpected legal or regulatory issues — 103
   7. Burnout - Small business owners often wear many hats and have to handle various tasks, leading to burnout — 109
   8. No online presence - A strong online presence is crucial in today's market — 114
   9. Employee turnover - Rapid employee turnover can be detrimental to a small business — 120
   10. Lack of innovation - Failing to innovate can lead to a small business becoming outdated — 125
   11. Poor time management - Poor time management can lead to missed opportunities and a lack of productivity — 132
   12. Lack of Systems & Processes — 136
   13. Other factors that contribute to business failure — 141

5. **The Solutions - What Can Be Done to Reduce Business Failure?** — **144**

Conclusion — 156
10 Inspirational Quotes About Failure — 159
Appendices — 161
References — 162
Acknowledgements — 166

About Chris Beks

Chris is a local Small Business Expert with over 40 years of experience, a qualified Accountant, Mortgage Broker, Financial Planner, International Best-selling Author, Business Coach, and Team Leader at the multi-award-winning Ceebeks Business Solutions for GOOD.

He started his business journey as an accountant after graduating in 1983, and launched Ceebeks Business Solutions for GOOD in 1990. Ceebeks Business Solutions' purpose is *'to positively impact the lives of young families in business to make their businesses really work, so that together we can make an even bigger impact in our communities, country, and the lives of those less fortunate around the world.'*

Today, he has a small Team – 'The Sensational Seven' – who provide their multi-award-winning services to customers across Australia.

Chris is the best-selling business co-author of **Legacy: The Sustainable Development Goals in Action**, which he co-wrote with 52 business and community leaders from around the world. He published the first of his series of business books, **Chasing the Dream - How to Grow a Business in these Amazing Times** in 2019, and **Starting the Dream** is the second book in this series, with **Realising the Dream** to be launched in 2024.

He is a very proud father of three adult daughters Dinah, Alli and Sofie, partner of Angela, and lives in Warrnambool with their Golden Retriever, Frankie, Burmese cats, Delilah and Daisy, and ten chooks. Chris is a passionate gardener, trying to create a tropical oasis in a temperate climate, a beekeeper, early morning gym enthusiast, and tenor with the Cindy Lee Ensemble, who often perform at charity events and fundraisers.

Preface

Starting the Dream! - *How to Avoid a Nightmare When You Start a Business* is the sequel or antithesis to my first book, **Chasing the Dream** - *How to Grow a Business in these Amazing Times* that came out during the COVID pandemic to help struggling businesses get back on their feet.

Starting the Dream! is an indispensable guide for anyone who is looking to start a business. With the rapidly changing business landscape and the growing number of entrepreneurs entering the market, it's more important than ever to be well-informed and equipped with the right tools and strategies to succeed.

This book is designed to help aspiring entrepreneurs understand the more common reasons why businesses fail, and provide them with the knowledge and resources they need to avoid these pitfalls.

Through a combination of expert insights, practical advice, and real-world case studies gathered over my 40+ years' experience as an Accountant and Business Advisor, **Starting the Dream!** provides a comprehensive roadmap for success.

The examples in this book come from real-life businesses, whose names and locations across the country have been changed for privacy reasons.

Whether you're just starting out or have been in business for a while, this book is the essential guide you need to build a solid foundation and achieve long-term success. So don't wait another day to avoid the nightmare in starting the business of your dreams.

Start reading today, and learn from your copy of **Starting the Dream!** - *How to Avoid a Nightmare When You Start a Business today!*

Chris Beks
Small business champion, entrepreneur, author,
mentor & life explorer

The Setting

- Economic necessity is the motivating reason for starting a business.
- Most entrepreneurs have an 'entrepreneurial seizure' to start a business based on the technical skills they have acquired, but no real idea of what is required to run and manage a successful business.
- For others, going into business is forced upon them by being laid off, redundancy, spouse illness, mental health issues, wanting to break the monotony of working nine-to-five in a boring job, or following their passion
- Successful ones have a vision, a purpose, understand why, and have a higher calling to succeed, which involves continual education, outsourcing, systemizing, and getting professional advice from the outset.
- Purpose of the book: to help educate wannabe small business owners about the issues that those who have trod the path before them faced, and why their businesses failed. And to increase their chances of success by looking at ways to reduce any likelihood of failure.

The Characters

Dreamers who are passionate about their ideas and want to start a business

Wannabe entrepreneurs – solopreneurs, mumprenurs, seniorpreneurs and XYZpreneurs

Experienced tradies, managers, executives with dreams of a better and more balanced life

Self-employed business owners of various types, sizes and industries, who want to shift from being shackled to the business - working in it - to working on it to realise their dream.

Plot

Small businesses are essential to every economy; they play various vital roles contributing to the country's economic growth and well-being. Not only do small businesses provide more jobs, they also support careers and create opportunities across all communities. Successful small businesses put money back into their local community through wages and taxes, which can then support the creation of new small businesses and improve local public services.

However, most small businesses shut down within three years. According to data from the Bureau of Labor Statistics, as reported by Fundera, approximately 20% of small businesses fail within the first year. By the end of the second year, 30% of businesses will have failed. By the end of the fifth year, about half will have failed. And by the end of the decade, only 30% of businesses will remain — a 70% failure rate, costing their 'new' owners billions in lost income, sleepless nights, their health and sometimes their family!

Over the course of my 40+ years as an accountant and business adviser, I've learnt there are several reasons why. The principal ones are:

- Lack of leadership
- Poor management
- Lack of market research
- Financial problems (predominantly lack of sustainable cash flow and ability to manage it)
- Weak governance structures
- Problems with product/service and poor implementation of strategies
- External factors such as a change in government policies.

Despite these challenges, some small businesses have succeeded for years by:

- Developing a sound plan and sticking to it
- Having accountable and responsible leaders
- Taking appropriate measures to improve quality, value, and uniqueness of a product/service to suit market trends
- Developing a sound product/service model
- Practising financial discipline.

Given market conditions, and if supply and demand rules hold, why do so many small businesses fail so quickly and how can you avoid being one of them?

Foreword

Starting a business is often seen as the realisation of a dream, a step towards independence and success. However, all too often this dream turns into a harsh reality—a nightmare of wasted time, energy, and money. The statistics are daunting: over 60% of small businesses fail within three years. It's a staggering number that highlights the urgent need for guidance and knowledge before taking the leap into entrepreneurship.

In **Starting the Dream!** *How to Avoid a Nightmare When You Start a Business*, Chris Beks presents a vital resource that every aspiring entrepreneur should read before embarking on their journey. Drawing from over 40 years of practical experience and a deep understanding of the challenges that lie ahead, his book unveils the key tools, processes, and insights that have propelled thousands of small businesses to success.

Too often, individuals enter the business world relying solely on their technical skills, unaware of the complexities involved in setting up, running, and managing a business. This lack of preparation and understanding can have far-reaching consequences, impacting not only the business itself but also the lives of those involved. That's why it is crucial to arm oneself with knowledge before diving into the unknown.

Within the pages of **Starting the Dream!** you will embark on a transformative journey, one that will equip you with essential knowledge and guide you towards building a solid foundation for your business. Chris shares invaluable lessons learned from both successes and failures, which may spare you some painful experiences. By learning from the mistakes of others, you avoid common pitfalls and fast-track your progress towards sustainable success.

From the importance of establishing a clear and separate business structure to understanding your responsibilities and liabilities, this book delves into the fundamental aspects that underpin a thriving enterprise. It underlines the significance of fruitful delegation, helping you recognise that you cannot—and should not—attempt to do it all on your own. The exploration of leadership and management skills serves as a reminder that your role extends beyond your technical expertise, and that the success of your business hinges on your ability to guide and inspire your Team.

Market research is unveiled as a critical component in understanding your target audience, their needs, and how to position your business for success. By delving into this aspect, you will gain the insights necessary to make informed decisions and seize opportunities that align with your goals. **Starting the Dream!** emphasises the importance of tracking your key numbers, enabling you to monitor progress, identify areas for improvement, and ensure the financial health of your venture.

Finally, **Starting the Dream!** focuses on the transformative power of planning and systemising your business. By developing coherent strategies and implementing efficient processes, you lay the groundwork for long-term profitability and sustainable growth. The author offers practical advice and actionable steps, empowering you to build a resilient business that can weather the storms and provide support, not only for you but for your loved ones and employees.

As you embark on your journey of entrepreneurship, remember the wisdom shared within these pages, and recognise that seeking advice and assistance from professionals and those around you is not a sign of weakness, but an indispensable step towards building a healthy, successful business. You are not alone in this endeavour, and the insights found in this book will equip you to navigate the challenges and seize the opportunities that lie ahead.

Prepare yourself for the adventure of a lifetime. **Starting the Dream!** *How to Avoid a Nightmare When You Start a Business* is your compass, your guiding light through the uncharted waters of entrepreneurship. Learn from the experiences of others, embrace the knowledge presented, and set sail towards the realisation of your dreams.

Remember, the journey may be challenging, but armed with the right tools and insights, you can transform your dream into a resounding success. May this book be your steadfast companion as you embark on this exhilarating journey, and may your entrepreneurial spirit soar to new heights.

Jaqui Lane
Serial book publishing entrepreneur, author, mentor, lifelong learner

Introduction

There are various definitions of a small business, but one thing is clear: there is no universally accepted definition. No single description of a small business will suit both the government and the private sector. The usual definitions preferred, for instance, in Australia consider the revenue turnover or the number of people employed, or both. In this regard, according to the Australian Bureau of Statistics (ABS), 2018, small businesses are the ones engaging in active trading with 0-19 employees.

The ABS indicates that there are 2.1 million small businesses in Australia, and they are the backbone of the economy. In South Australia, for example, small businesses are the major employers and exporters (Frost, 2019).

Despite this fact, starting, running, and keeping these businesses afloat is never smooth sailing.

One of the daily mysteries facing the individuals running them is the reason for their failure - why some entrepreneurs start one successful business after another, while others cannot even kick-start one.

Why?

1
What the statistics tell us about business failures

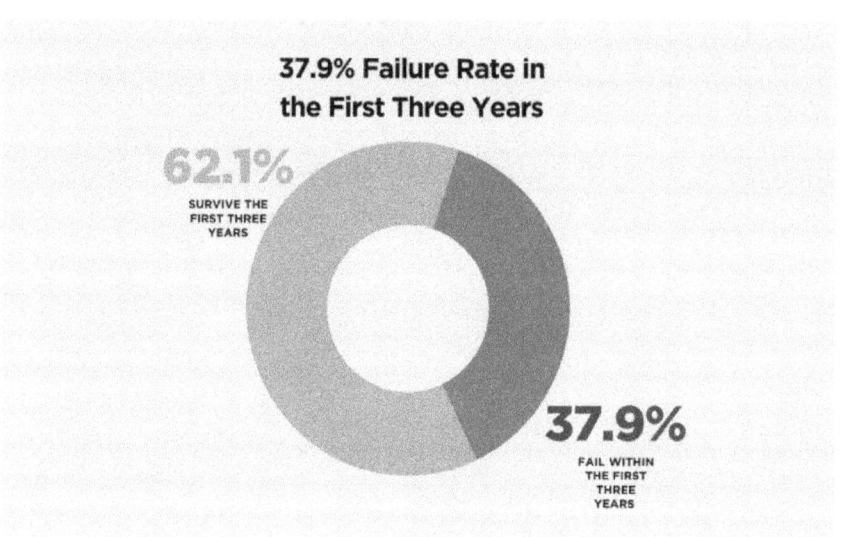

The Australian Bureau of Statistics indicates that over 60% of small businesses cease operating within three years of starting.

It is a daunting figure, and something that is thrown at the most enthusiastic business individual who announces to the world that he or she is about to start a new venture. It's also an extremely sad and largely avoidable statistic. These small businesses account for the overwhelming majority of businesses in Australia, representing 97% of all companies, and it's clear they're shutting their doors in alarmingly high numbers (ABS, 2018).

And this was before the global COVID pandemic between 2020 and 2022.

According to the September 2021 Bulletin published by the Reserve Bank of Australia, small businesses have been disproportionately affected by the COVID-19 pandemic, because they are more likely to be in industries that have been harder hit by restrictions on people movement, such as cafés, restaurants, the arts, and recreation. Many of them never recovered - some were struggling to survive before the pandemic and were finally pushed over the edge, while others were simply crippled with no customers or cash flow, and no way out except closure.

COVID aside, according to research conducted by the Small Business Administration of Australia, only half of small businesses are still operating beyond five years, and only a third see it through the ten-year mark.

What is even more shocking is the fact that 65% of new small businesses don't operate for ten years (Burns, 2016). Based on Bloomberg research, Forbes reports that eight out of ten new small businesses have failed within 18 months.

So, how do you make sure you're one of 33% still thriving after ten years?

Read on.

2
Beginning: Why go into business?

No one has ever started a business to fail on purpose.
   In fact, I could nearly guarantee that all start-ups and new business owners were full of positivity and optimism at the beginning - failure was probably pushed to the back of their

minds because it was swamped by this consuming passion, and the challenge to do something new.

The idea of running your own business is often accompanied by great excitement - and for good reason, as it can offer some great perks. Many entrepreneurs are overly excited at the prospect of starting a business and becoming masters of their own destiny - the CEO of 'My Own Company Pty Ltd' - but are ignorant of just what is required and the actual risks involved.

Deciding to start your own business requires a huge a leap of faith, because you are leaving behind the known - a regular pay cheque, work colleagues, the daily rituals, the consistent never-ending work cycle, and replacing it with the unknown:

- Who will work with me?
- Where will my next sale come from?
- How will I pay the bills?
- What do I need to do this properly?
- Which tools/apps work best?
- When will I make a profit?
- Why don't my numbers make sense?

It requires pushing out of your comfort zone and trying something new.

If that idea excites you, why wait? You're ready to take the leap and be the CEO of your OWN COMPANY. It's a lot of work and there are some risks, but the potential for rewards is huge.

So why do people go into business?

There are many reasons why, and let's look at these in a little more detail:

Economic necessity - loss of employment, preserve job (take over from boss)

Sometimes businesses are started or born out of the need to 'put food on the table and pay the bills' because of a forced redundancy, economic circumstances or an unprecedented global pandemic like COVID.

The skill set of the entrepreneur has allowed them to hire out their services, create or market products to sell or the expertise to solve problems to make life easier for others. This is way more prevalent today as COVID and the rapid advancement in technology have allowed thousands of new businesses to pop up in what is called the 'gig economy' - a labour market characterised by lots of small, short-term contracts or freelance work as opposed to permanent jobs.

Other new business owners have had entrepreneurship thrust upon them with the sudden illness or death of their boss, where to keep their job they have taken over the business.

Entrepreneurial seizure

I met Michael Gerber in Melbourne in the late '90s not too long after I had started my business. He was on a worldwide tour to promote his best-selling book **The E-Myth Revisited - Why**

Most Small Businesses Don't Work and What to Do About It, and he spoke about how most people, just like you and me, probably suffered an *'entrepreneurial seizure'!*

'My boss is an idiot', 'If it weren't for me this place wouldn't exist', 'Anybody can run a business, and I'll guarantee you I can do it better than the people upstairs'.

And so they quit their job to start a business that will give them a lifestyle, freedom, and the money to do what they want to do.

The assumption that they make is that they understand the business because they understand – and maybe are experts at – the technical side of the business. They think because they know their work, they are qualified to run the business.

But this could not be further from the truth!

Then reality sets in, and they're 'doing it, doing it, doing it all ', and instead of creating utopia for themselves they have created a business hell - they have created a **NIGHTMARE!**

By starting their own business, they move from a job they are very capable, maybe even fantastic, at to the same role plus 20 others which they know almost nothing about.

After the convulsions are over and the smoke has cleared, what is left? A would-be entrepreneur with the skills of a technician, now a part of the business world – and in trouble - big, big trouble!

Have you seen, firsthand, examples of this?

I'm willing to bet you either have known or do know someone like that, because it really is so common.

You know, your girlfriend - the hairdresser who quit her job last year to start her own salon - or your mate - the plumber who told his boss to stick it about six months ago and started his own plumbing business? No longer do you get to see them as frequently as you would like to, because they are flat out trying to keep up with all the aspects of running a business – managing cash flow, chasing up debtors, answering the phone, making appointments, instructing and leading Team Members, scheduling work, doing the work, sending out invoices, preparing marketing campaigns, etc.

In the words of Michael Gerber – they're 'doing it, doing it, doing it!'

Break the nine-to-five monotony

When I was growing up way back in the '60s and '70s, we had been conditioned by society and trained to think that we must go to school, get good grades, then head off to university, and finally get a stable desk job to be 'happy' and to 'get anywhere in this world"! Now, some of that might be true, but the end goal of working behind a desk from nine-to-five is not for everyone. Yes, there may be some people who crave and love the stability and routine of a nine-to-five work-life balance, but many of those jobs don't exist any more, and the online platform revolution has led to the gig economy. And now with the evolution of AI (artificial intelligence), many more jobs will no longer exist, and be replaced by ones that haven't even been created yet!

The initial excitement and novelty of starting your first job eventually wears off, and you are left with either the satisfaction of coming into work and doing what you love, or days of feeling unhappy, unfulfilled, unappreciated, and unsettled. It might take some time to realise that being in the office and behind a desk day in, day out is the one thing making you hate your job.

A monotonous day can crush even the most positive of spirits.

Whether you are working for someone else or for yourself, it will always require a certain level of reporting, documenting, data entry, and number crunching. Unfortunately, business is business and it requires paperwork - especially paperwork that is 100% accurate, on time, and up to date!

Although in business you can hire, delegate, and outsource the boring monotonous parts that you don't want to do, that doesn't mean that you can then ignore them.

Understanding the key numbers that make your business tick is critical to its survival - just like the gauges on the dashboard of your car give you critical information such as fuel level, speed, temperature, etc.

Follow your passion

Many entrepreneurs start their own business to follow their dreams and fulfill their passion, and this was most certainly the case for me way back when I started on the 26th May 1990.

I am a first-generation Australian, and my Dutch family were given an opportunity to start a new life in Australia after leaving behind their war-ravaged homeland razed by the Nazis during World War II. My father couldn't speak English when he arrived as a 20-year-old, and his lack of understanding how money worked – investing, borrowing and budgeting meant that we lived pay packet to pay packet, and it must have been a real financial struggle raising us seven kids! But my Mum was a miracle worker, and could stretch Dad's pay so far that we attended private school, played sports, and always had regular meals - even though I would never, ever choose to eat some of those dishes again.

My dream was to find out why people who had their own business were often more financially successful than those who didn't. I found in secondary school that I liked business maths and accounting. My Year 12 teacher, Sister Marg, told me 'Mr Beks, if you ever decide to be an accountant one day, you will be a very good one!" This was the start of making my dream come true. I wanted to use the knowledge of accounting and business I acquired to improve the quality of life of people who lacked this understanding and education.

After graduating in 1983, I initially started working for a large regional accounting firm as a 'Boy Friday', making coffee, running errands, checking and filing - and was extremely frustrated as my Bachelor of Business and Graduate Diploma in Management Accounting degrees were not being put to good use.

I moved to Melbourne in 1985, and joined international accounting firm Ernst & Whinney, now EY Australia, where my boss saw that I was not only a quick learner, but also hungry to learn new things. When the business services division was quiet, I was moved to the insolvency division, and when they were quiet I had a stint in audit and tax, etc. I was given an opportunity to experience and learn many facets of accounting and business during this two-year 'intensive' that would have not been achievable in any country accounting firm - or would have taken me at least 15 years to accumulate had I remained.

I returned to Warrnambool in the south-west of Victoria in 1987, and worked in a couple of local firms, where I quickly became disillusioned, because they lacked ethics and were more concerned with their lifestyles and appearances than making a difference to the welfare of their customers.

I 'hung up my shingle' in 1990, and have invested thousands of dollars in courses, seminars and conferences over many years to become well educated in running a business, and able to teach those same lessons to other business owners. And I continue to invest in learning to improve my business and pass on knowledge and insights to our customers.

Today Ceebeks Business Solutions for GOOD is a multi-award-winning business, recognised worldwide for its impacts on the lives of those less fortunate. We are on a mission of making 30 million global impacts which change the lives of those less fortunate by 2030, the date set by the United Nations in 2015 to end poverty and hunger everywhere - to combat inequalities within and among countries, to build peaceful, just, and inclusive societies, to protect human rights and promote gender equality and the empowerment of women and girls, and to ensure the lasting protection of the planet and its natural resources. We are closing in on 13 million impacts in the form of clean water, goats for farming, books for education, toilets etc at the time of writing this book.

Following your dreams and living your passion will fulfill you in a way that working for someone else may not do. You are in charge of creating your business from the ground up - a business that is based on your vision and purpose - one that you can mould and shape to give you the work-life balance you're after. It can help you achieve greater financial independence and be something you're proud of, and that you may even be able to pass on as your legacy to your children.

And speaking of your legacy, it will allow you to create a legacy that you can experience and live while you are alive, rather than something you don't experience when you're gone!

2. BEGINNING: WHY GO INTO BUSINESS?

3
Why running a business can be a nightmare

Running a small business can become a nightmare for a variety of reasons, including a lack of predictable, consistent cash flow, absence of customers, intense competition, new competitors, poor management, insufficient financial and tax knowledge, or unknown or unexpected legal or regulatory issues.

Also, small business owners often wear many hats and must handle multiple roles and tasks such as accounting, marketing, and operations. Often these are not skills the business owner has, so they have to learn on the job, which can quickly lead to burnout and the business spiraling out of control.

This is the 'hell' that Michael Gerber refers to, and it can take a huge toll on the health of the business owner. According to the December 2022 report Small Business and Mental Health - Through the Pandemic, there were high levels of mental ill-health within the small business sector with 22% of small business respondents - just over one in five - reporting having been diagnosed with a mental ill-health condition by a doctor or health professional, and in some industry groups the figures were higher at around one in three. A key cause of stress for small business owners was finding a balance between the demands of work, family, and personal life following the COVID-19 lockdowns. The fact that the stigma associated with mental ill-health is still an issue doesn't help those who suffer, with 46% of respondents thinking they would be treated poorly if they disclosed they had been diagnosed with a mental illness. Not only that, but barriers to accessing support include the cost (54%), lack of time (49%), and services not understanding the needs of small businesses (39%).

The health impacts on a small business owner if their business is turning into a nightmare can be serious. Possible impacts include:

1. **Stress:** Running a small business can be very stressful and, if the business is not doing well, even overwhelming. High levels of stress can lead to physical and mental problems such as headaches, high blood pressure, depression, and anxiety.
2. **Lack of sleep:** Small business owners may have to work long hours and sacrifice sleep in order to keep afloat. Lack of sleep can lead to fatigue, irritability, and decreased productivity.
3. **Poor diet and physical activity:** Small business owners may not have the time or energy to take care of themselves properly, and may neglect their diet and physical activity. This can lead to weight gain, poor nutrition, and a host of health problems.
4. **Isolation:** Small business owners may feel isolated and alone, especially if they are the only employee or running various virtual contractors/suppliers/workers. Social isolation can lead to depression and anxiety.
5. **Burnout:** Small business owners may feel exhausted and overwhelmed by the demands of running a business. Burnout can lead to physical and emotional exhaustion, cynicism, and detachment from work.

It is important as small business owners that you recognise the possible health impacts of running a business, and take steps to prioritise your well-being. This may include seeking support from friends and family, finding healthy ways to manage stress, and taking time off when necessary to rest and recharge.

By implementing healthy stress management techniques and allowing themselves adequate time off to rest and recharge, small business owners can protect their physical and mental health.

I can speak about this first-hand as I have a regular morning fitness ritual that involves getting up at 4:50 am, drinking pre-workout supplement, completing 100 pushups, and stretching my over-60-year-old limbs, all in readiness for my one-hour gym class. I also try to get at least seven to eight hours of sleep each night. I have managed to stay relatively flu-free, fit and sharp for the day ahead, and just love the benefits I get from doing this daily.

Here are some tips and resources to help small business owners to manage stress and take time off when necessary:

1. Practise self-care:

- **Take regular exercise:** Physical activity releases endorphins, reduces stress hormones, and promotes overall well-being. Find activities you enjoy, such as walking, yoga, or swimming, and make them a part of your routine.
- **Prioritise sleep:** Aim for seven to eight hours of quality sleep each night. Establish a relaxing bedtime routine and create a comfortable sleep environment.
- **Eat a balanced diet:** Nourish your body with wholesome meals and snacks. Avoid excessive caffeine and sugar, as they can contribute to stress and energy crashes.

- **Engage in activities you enjoy:** Dedicate time to hobbies, interests, and spending time with loved ones. Engaging in pleasurable activities helps reduce stress and improves overall satisfaction.

2. Practice Stress Reduction Techniques:

- **Deep breathing exercises:** Take slow, deep breaths and focus on your breath. This can help calm your mind and reduce stress.
- **Mindfulness and meditation:** Incorporate mindfulness practices such as mindful breathing, body scans, or guided meditation into your daily routine. These can improve your ability to manage stress.
- **Time management:** Prioritise tasks, delegate responsibilities when possible, and break large projects into smaller, more manageable tasks. Efficient time management reduces stress and increases productivity.
- **Set boundaries:** Establish clear boundaries between work and personal life. Avoid overworking, and allow yourself time for relaxation and rejuvenation.

3. Seek Support and Assistance:

- **Friends and family:** Share your concerns and challenges with trusted friends and family members. They can provide emotional support and offer valuable perspectives.

- **Networking and mentorship:** Join local business networks or industry-specific groups to connect with fellow small business owners who may have faced similar challenges. Mentors can offer guidance and support based on their experience.
- **Small business associations and chambers of commerce:** These organisations often provide resources, training programs, and networking opportunities specifically designed to support small business owners.
- **Business advisory services:** Seek advice from business consultants or coaches who specialise in supporting small business owners. They can provide guidance on various aspects of running a business, and help you navigate challenges.

4. Take Time Off:

- **Plan regular breaks:** Schedule short breaks throughout your workday to relax, stretch, or engage in enjoyable activities. These breaks can help you recharge and maintain productivity.
- **Holiday time:** Plan and take vacations to disconnect from work completely. Use this time to rest, spend quality time with loved ones, and engage in activities that bring you joy.
- **Delegate responsibilities:** Train and empower your employees or consider outsourcing certain tasks to trusted

professionals. Delegating responsibilities can help lighten your workload and provide you with more opportunities for time off.

There are organisations in Australia that provide help, support and guidance; here are some of those:
- **Small Business Development Corporation (SBDC):** Provides resources, training programs, and advice for small business owners. Visit their website at www.smallbusiness.wa.gov.au
- **Australian Small Business and Family Enterprise Ombudsman:** Offers support and assistance to small business owners, including dispute resolution services. Their website is www.asbfeo.gov.au
- **Beyond Blue:** Provides mental health support and resources for individuals and businesses. Their website offers information and access to counselling services at www.beyondblue.org.au
- **Small Business Support Line:** Operated by the Australian government, this helpline offers free and confidential support, advice, and referral services for small business owners. You can reach them at 13 28 46 or visit their website at www.smallbusiness.wa.gov.au
- **Business Victoria:** Provides resources, workshops, and support programs for small business owners in Victoria. Visit their website at www.business.vic.gov.au for more information.

- **Ceebeks Business Solutions for GOOD:** 40 years of experience in dealing with Accounting, Tax, Financial Planning, Mortgage Broking & Business Coaching. Visit their website at www.ceebeks.com for more information.

Remember, as a small business owner, your well-being is essential for the success and sustainability of your business. By adopting healthy stress management strategies, seeking support when needed, and prioritising rest and recharge, you can maintain a healthy work-life balance and thrive in both your personal and professional life. Take care of yourself, and your business will benefit from your improved well-being.

4
The Causes - what are the reasons why business fail?

The worst and most humiliating fact about businesses failing is that the entrepreneur is unaware until it is too late (Sampagnaro, Meles, & Verdoliva, 2015). If they knew the reason in time, they would make an effort to salvage the business and keep it running, but sometimes no amount of effort will change the outcome.

4. THE CAUSES - WHAT ARE THE REASONS WHY BUSINESS FAIL?

Most entrepreneurs live in denial or are even unaware of the mistakes they are making (Storey, 2016). The journey in this respect is unforgiving. The challenges are constant, with moving variables involved, each of which could put you out of business at any point (Westrenius, & Barnes, 2015).

So then, what are the factors contributing to small business failure if there was given an equal chance of survival and same levels of demand for the products or services?

In 2018, the Australian Centre for Business Growth published research which identified the reasons Australian Small Medium Enterprises (SMEs) fail. The research was the first of its kind, and the processes involved senior management whose organisations had failed, or were part of businesses that failed. The findings identified the following elements that had contributed significantly to business failure:

1. Lack of leadership and management skills, including poor planning, insufficient market research and sales skills, mismanagement of financials, underestimating the impact of externalities, and weak governance structures
2. The inability to conduct research or understand the market or sales perspective of their industry
3. Lack of finance skills and reliance on other people for the financial health of the organisation
4. Lack of enough knowledge of the proper ways to fund the institution

5. The impact of the externalities. Most people blindsided by changes in regulations, interest rates, drought, fire or global trends among others did not have a proper and sound risk mitigation plan in place
6. Weak governance structures - systems that outline how a business is managed and controlled
7. Problems associated with family members or partners, leading to the collapse of a relationship.

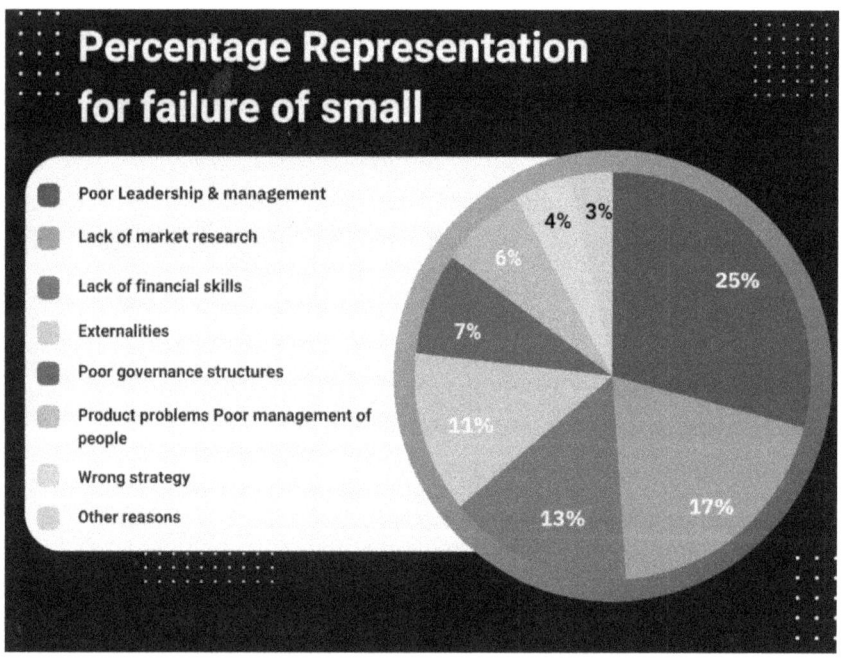

Table 1. Percentage representation on reasons why small businesses fail

Reasons Why Small Businesses Fail

Let's look at some of the main reasons why small businesses fail, and what you can do to avoid your business failing:

1. Not seeking Professional Advice before starting

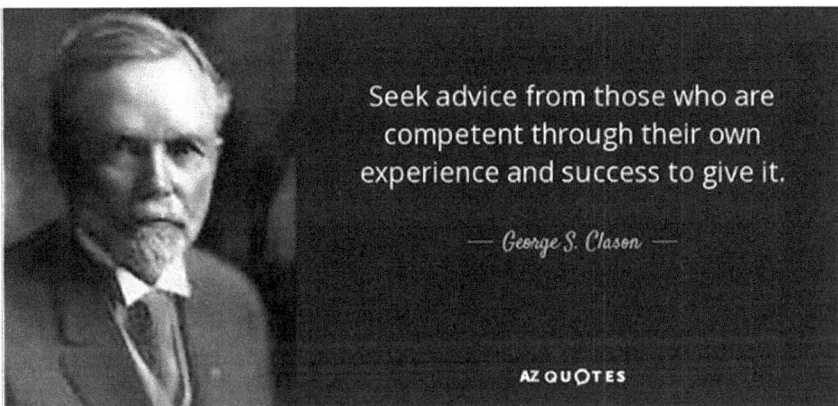

A key reason why so many small businesses fail is because they don't access and use established business and governance structures. Poor or non-existent governance structures and sour partnerships will create problems with family. Just what governance structures am I referring to?

Here's a short, basic list:
i) Company structure, ownership and shareholder agreements
ii) Company registration requirements
iii) Tax registration and reporting

iv) Partnership agreement
v) Intellectual property protection
vi) Privacy
vii) Directors and their responsibilities, payment, etc.

It is essential that you have sound governance structures in place. As the owner you should consult with professionals on tax requirements, company structures, proprieties, and other fundamentals affecting your business. These will vary depending on what type of business you are operating and in what sector. For example, the registration requirements for a hairdresser are different to those for an electrician or a builder as are the insurances, rates of pay, hours of work, and more.

Similarly, internally, a sound and simple organisational structure with clear roles and responsibilities should be established, communicated, and monitored. There must be complementary operational and procedural systems in place (job descriptions, KPIs/OKRs, reporting lines and frequency, OH&S policies, HR policies, and more) to ensure optimal productivity at all times.

It is often the little things that make a big difference.

It's important to have a Succession Plan and an Emergency Plan. Future leaders should be identified and gradually given more responsibility and authority if you have employees. If you don't you, need to think through and plan what will happen when you aren't there – either by design or accident. Without an definite Succession Plan, you and your company are unprepared to fill openings created by retirement, unexpected departures, or death.

Most people don't realise that starting a business is like going to the casino and putting your house on red.

Starting a business is a risk - a huge risk.

A risk because success is not guaranteed, and unless you take certain precautions to reduce your exposure to this risk you could end up losing your house. Many small business owners before you have, and continue to do so.

The Sad Case of Jane Doe

Jane and her husband came to see us almost a decade ago about buying some property interstate. We spoke with them about

limiting their risk by structuring the purchase in a separate legal entity and having adequate Life and Total Permanent Disability insurances in their superannuation funds to ensure that if a life event were to occur then the insurance proceeds would clear the mortgages they had on their home and this investment property, and leave a sufficient lump sum to help them raise their seven kids.

Jane didn't believe in superannuation and contributing to it. 'We can make more money with property.' I can still clearly hear her response to my question 'What if you or John couldn't work anymore or died? 'Whoever is left can just sell the investment property and pay off the mortgages.' Several years passed, and interest rates were quite high when Jane suffered a medical episode and died. John had to pick up the pieces as best he could, but was finally forced from the family home due to the bank's foreclosure as the investment property could not be sold. John and his family lost everything: their investments, home, spouse and mother.

Starting a business can be a complex and challenging task, and not seeking professional advice beforehand may have serious consequences, including business failure. There are several reasons why seeking professional advice is essential to business success. Below are some examples that accentuate the importance of seeking professional advice.

- **Lack of knowledge and experience:** You may not be aware of important legal requirements, such as registering the business or obtaining the necessary licenses and permits. This can result in costly penalties and legal difficulties, and can even lead to the business being shut down.
- **Inappropriate business structure:** Setting up the business in the wrong business structure can result in a lack of opportunities to minimise and pay less tax, and expose the business owners to the risk of losing their assets as well as opportunities lost to take advantage of government grants. Some government incentives require a company structure only.

- **Inadequate planning and preparation:** You may not fully understand the market, the competition, and your target audience, which can lead to poor decisions and ineffective, costly marketing strategies. In addition, you may not have a clear understanding of your business model, which can result in a lack of focus and direction, and eventually failure.
- **Financial mismanagement:** You may not be aware of the importance of budgeting, forecasting, and financial tracking, which can result in poor decision-making and ultimately financial mismanagement. Not understanding that you are 'pseudo-tax collectors' for the ATO, where the GST paid to you by your customers to hand over to the ATO at the end of the reporting period is your responsibility and not extra revenue for you to spend can lead to cash flow problems, an inability to pay the ATO when required, unexpected bills and salaries, and even bankruptcy.
- **Limited network and resources:** Working with a professional adviser can help you expand your network and access valuable resources. For example, Ceebeks Business Solutions for GOOD is part of a worldwide business network and connects entrepreneurs with prospective investors, customers, and suppliers, which can help businesses grow and succeed locally, nationally and globally. Without such connections, you may struggle to get the support and resources you need to succeed.

Our Solution - seek professional advice before starting a business

The investment you make before starting a business is a form of insurance - insurance against risking and losing everything you currently have. From understanding your risk position, structuring to protect your family home and other assets, having a business and marketing plan to understand where you want to go and how to get there to strategies on how to hang on to more of the profits without, in the words of the late Kerry Packer, 'donating it to the Government'.

> **Chasers Tip**
> Getting professional advice is essential for success. Entrepreneurs who do not seek professional advice risk making costly mistakes, encountering legal difficulties, and ultimately facing business failure.

2. **Financial instability** - This can be described as a lack of proper financial planning and management and can lead to financial instability, which can cause a small business to fail.

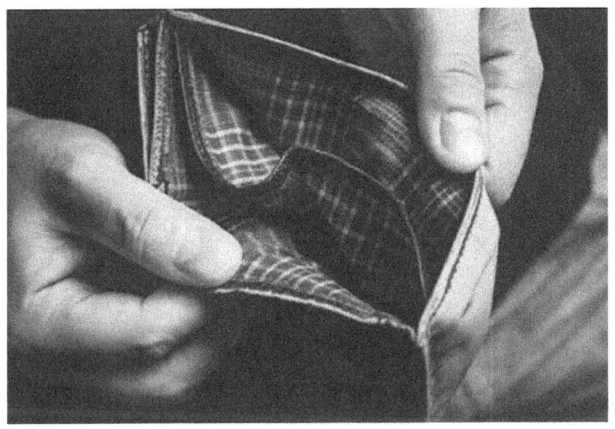

One factor is repeatedly identified as the reason for small businesses shutting their doors. Credit reporting agency illion estimated that 90% of failed Australian small businesses did so due to poor cash flow and its management. Incredibly, a good business, one that is both profitable and growing, can go under because of a mismatch in the timing of when your bills must be paid and when your customers are not paying you. As the director of a company, you have a legal responsibility to pay your bills 'as and when they come due'. If you can't, and don't make arrangements with your creditors, you can be 'trading while insolvent'. This means you can become personally liable for the debts of your company. Ouch!

The Australian Centre for Business Growth reports 14% of respondents admitting to failure of small enterprises because of poor financial management, especially concerning working capital, management, and profitability (Dwyer & Kotey, p.117, 2015). In reality, this seems much more relevant than the financial skills on a balance sheet or strategic finance, planning, or even analysis. The main reason is **that the flow of cash in every organisation is like air for business operations.** It needs careful attention, micro-planning, and a view of the longer-term goals. Traditional lenders are a helpful resource for cash flow, but the time it takes to get finance is often the difference between sink and sail.

Various studies also indicate that most of the businesses do not make a profit. According to Small Business Trends, only 40% of small businesses are profitable, and 30% break even, while the other 30% are losing money. **Revenue is not the same as profit.** As an entrepreneur, you must keep an eye on the driving factor, profitability, at all times. Gain allows for growth (Julien, 2018). In this respect, the business enthusiast should know how to put a correct price tag on an item or a service - having communicated and tested the same price. Throwing out a price at customers without a balance of value can turn them away from your business or allow them to buy your product or service at a loss to you.

Revenue refers to the total amount of money a business earns from its operations, while profit represents the amount of money left after deducting all expenses from the revenue.

Let's look at two businesses operating in different industries to understand the difference between revenue and profit.

We will explore a scenario where Business A generates considerable revenue but little or no profit, while Business B has low revenue but a healthy profit.

Business A: E-Commerce Retailer

Business A sells a wide range of products online. They have a large customer base and charge competitive prices, resulting in a heavy volume of sales. Let's analyse their financial situation:

> **Revenue:** Business A's revenue is impressive, with millions of dollars generated annually. The company's products are in great demand, and they attract a many customers due to successful marketing strategies and competitive pricing.

> **Expenses:** However, Business A faces several challenges that eat into their revenue. They incur hefty expenses in various areas, including:

1. **Inventory Costs:** Business A needs to maintain a large inventory to meet customer demand. This requires large-scale investment and ongoing expenses for warehousing, logistics, and inventory management.
2. **Marketing and Advertising:** To attract a large customer base, they invest heavily in marketing and advertising

campaigns. These expenses include online advertisements, search engine optimization, and social media promotions.
3. **Fulfillment and Shipping:** As an e-commerce retailer, they must fulfill customer orders promptly and efficiently. This involves costs associated with packaging, shipping, and customer service.
4. **Technology Infrastructure:** Maintaining a robust and secure e-commerce platform requires continuous investment in technology infrastructure, website development, and cybersecurity.
5. **Operating Expenses:** General administrative costs, employee salaries, rent for office space, and utilities contribute to the overall expenses.

Profit: Despite the impressive revenue, Business A struggles to generate a handsome profit due to the vast expenses. The combination of inventory costs, marketing expenditure, fulfillment expenses, technology infrastructure, and other operating costs significantly reduces their profit margin. Consequently, the business may end up with little or no profit despite the substantial revenue.

Business B: Specialised Consulting Firm

Business B offers niche services to a select clientele. Although their customer base is relatively small, their expertise and top-quality service position them as industry leaders. Let's examine their financial situation:

> **Revenue:** Business B's revenue is comparatively low compared to Business A. The specialised nature of their services means that they have a smaller target market. However, due to their exceptional reputation and expertise, they can command premium prices for their services.

> **Expenses:** Business B operates with a lean business model and incurs minimal expenses, including:

1. **Skilled Workforce:** The primary expense for Business B is the salaries of skilled consultants. Their expertise allows them to provide top-tier services to clients, but the cost of hiring and retaining such talent can be huge.
2. **Office Space and Utilities:** Business B requires a professional office space to conduct meetings and consultations. The costs of renting an office, utilities, and other related expenses are relatively modest.
3. **Marketing and Advertising:** Compared to Business A, Business B does not require extensive marketing and advertising. They rely primarily on word-of-mouth referrals,

industry partnerships, and targeted marketing to reach their niche clientele.

Profit: Despite their lower revenue, Business B enjoys high profit margins due to their low operating expenses. By focusing on providing specialised services to a select clientele, they can charge premium fees and maintain a healthy profit margin. Their minimal expenses and efficient operations allow them to achieve high profitability even with a relatively low revenue.

This example highlights the crucial difference between revenue and profit. Business A generates sizeable revenue through its e-commerce operations, attracting a large customer base and driving enormous sales volumes. However, their profit is compromised by considerable expenses such as inventory costs, marketing expenditure, fulfillment expenses, technology infrastructure, and other overheads. As a result, despite the high revenue, Business A struggles to generate a substantial profit.

On the other hand, Business B, despite having lower revenue, achieves high profitability due to its focused and specialised consulting services. By catering to a niche market and offering premium services, Business B can command higher prices and maintain a healthy profit margin. Their lean business model with minimal expenses allows them to maximise their profit even with a smaller customer base.

4. THE CAUSES - WHAT ARE THE REASONS WHY BUSINESS FAIL?

This example emphasises the importance of managing expenses to achieve profitability. Simply having high revenue does not guarantee profitability if expenses outpace the income generated. It underscores the need for businesses to analyse their cost structure carefully, identify areas for optimisation, and ensure that expenses are in line with the revenue generated.

Basically, both revenue and profit are essential indicators of a business's financial health. While high revenue can signify market success and customer demand, it is the profit that reflects the true viability and sustainability of a business. Striking the right balance between revenue generation and cost management is crucial for businesses to thrive and achieve long-term profitability.

Most businesses fail to develop and nurture a sound business model. That is, they operate without a Business Plan and pursue a business for which there is no proven revenue stream. It is difficult to scale when a business model isn't grounded. A clear channel to growth and development needs to be evident for your Team, customers, and (if you want) likely investors to buy in.

Management (whether that's just you or managers) must be responsible and keep records of all financial details, and always make decisions based on information from real data, such as:

- Number of new leads per day
- Conversion ratio (number of sales/number of leads)
- Cash in bank
- Bills due in 30 days
- Debts due in 30 days.

You need to know where the business stands all the time. If your people are not good with numbers, then it is best to hire a financial professional to explain and train you to at least understand the basics.

You must know, down to the last dollar, where the money in the business is coming from and where it's going for the entity to succeed. In a typical business, regardless of industry type, the key numbers/metrics you need to know should include the following:

- **Revenue:** The total amount of money generated from sales or services provided. It's crucial to track revenue to understand the financial health of the business.
- **Expenses:** The costs incurred in running the business, including rent, salaries, utilities, and other overheads. Monitoring expenses helps identify areas for cost control and efficiency improvements.
- **Gross Profit:** The difference between revenue and the direct costs associated with producing or delivering goods or services. Gross profit provides insight into the profitability of the core business operations.
- **Net Profit:** The amount remaining after deducting all expenses, including both direct and indirect costs, from the revenue. Net profit indicates the overall profitability of the business.
- **Cash Flow:** The movement of cash in and out of the business. Cash flow management is crucial for ensuring there is enough cash to cover expenses and invest in growth opportunities.

- **Accounts Receivable:** The amount of money owed to the business by customers or clients for goods or services provided on credit. Monitoring accounts receivable helps in tracking outstanding payments and managing cash flow.
- **Accounts Payable:** The amount of money the business owes to suppliers or vendors for goods or services received on credit. Keeping track of accounts payable is important for managing working capital and maintaining good relationships with suppliers.
- **Inventory Turnover:** The number of times inventory is sold or replaced within a given period. It helps assess the efficiency of inventory management and identify future issues, such as excess stock or slow-moving items.
- **Customer Acquisition Cost (CAC):** The amount of money spent on acquiring a new customer. Calculating CAC helps evaluate the value of marketing and sales efforts, and ensures that customer acquisition costs are in line with the revenue generated.
- **Customer Lifetime Value (CLV):** The total revenue generated from a customer over the entire duration of their relationship with the business. Understanding CLV helps in customer retention strategies and investment decisions.
- **Return on Investment (ROI):** The profitability of an investment relative to its cost. ROI helps evaluate the benefit of investments made in marketing, equipment, and other business activities.

- **Key Performance Indicators (KPIs):** These are specific metrics that vary depending on the nature of the business. They can include customer satisfaction, website traffic, conversion rates, employee productivity, and other relevant measures that align with the business goals.

By monitoring and analysing these key numbers and metrics, business owners can gain valuable insights into their business's financial performance, make informed decisions, and identify areas for improvement and growth...and be alerted to any signs of trouble ahead! Again, depending on your business model, sector, and structure, some of these numbers/data will be different from those listed above.

A business can also fail because of the lack of a 'rainy day plan' - *a reserve of money you can draw on when faced with financial challenges.* Most individuals start businesses with a dream of making money, but many lack financial skill on interest, taxes, expenses, cash flow, and other commercial matters. Lack of such skills puts a business on a path straight to failure. If they are to thrive and not just survive, business owners require skills in business and financial management – particularly planning and financial knowledge. Without these skills, they need external help and hands-on support to implement the necessary improvements (Journal of Small Business Management, 2015).

Financial instability can happen to any business, big or small, if proper financial planning and management is not in place. It refers to a situation where a business is unable to meet its financial obligations, such as paying its bills or loans, and may result in the business shutting down.

At times a business startup grows much faster than it can keep up with market requirements. For instance, you can open an online boutique with top trending clothes, and suddenly it is inundated with orders it is not able to fulfill. Or perhaps the opposite is true. People are so convinced that their products are going to take the world by storm that they invest heavily and order way too much inventory, and then cannot move it. Both of which result in a business failure. Before you enter a new market it is essential to maximise the existing market.

Maureen's Gift Store

Maureen* (not her real name) owned a small retail store, but she had a poor understanding of bookkeeping and did not keep accurate track of her expenses and income. As a consequence, she did not know how much money her business was making or losing, and quickly found that she might not be able to pay her bills on time, particularly the Tax Office. This led to late fees and penalties, which added up quickly and made it even harder for the store to stay afloat. When Maureen came to see us, she couldn't tell us how much money she owed or to whom. She couldn't tell us which stock items were profitable and which ones were 'chewing up' her profits. We set her business up with Xero - the best cloud accounting software designed for small businesses, in our opinion - and showed her how to watch the cost of goods sold so she didn't end up overstocking inventory, which was what had led to her cash flow problems.

If her accounting records had not been sorted quickly, and other management strategies put in place, Maureen would not have been able to afford to pay the rent, utilities or the salaries of her Team.

It took Maureen over 24 months to start driving her business towards profitability through active management of her business figures and attention to cash flow. She is now more aware of how to manage her business, and has a Team that helps her to do this.

Billy's

Fred owns a small restaurant called Billy's. He has never had enough cash on hand to cover unexpected expenses, such as a broken oven or a sudden drop in table numbers. Fred treated the business bank account like he'd won Tattslotto, drawing out more cash from the business for personal use than he needed to, and suddenly realised that he might have to close its doors when its oven and two refrigerators broke down through lack of maintenance. This would lead to a loss of revenue for several weeks and a large repair bill causing financial instability and severe strain on the restaurant's cash flow. Fortunately when he came to us, we were able to quickly secure business finance to temporarily cover the cash withdrawn by Fred to cover the repair bills, put in place a regular salary for him, and restore the business to prosperity.

Our Solutions - get advice on how to set up a solid accounting system, create a budget, forecast cash flow, and keep accurate financial records.

A cloud-based, collaborative accounting software like Xero allows you to capture the data immediately, identify the profitable items, and record the movement of stock, and also, at the touch of a button, to see how much is in the bank, how much is owing by whom, and how much is owed to whom!

To prevent financial instability, small business owners need to have a clear understanding of their financial situation by keeping accurate records of their income and expenses. As a business owner, you should also draw up a budget and stick to it, and have a plan in place for unexpected events. This means you should have a clear understanding of your income and expenses (weekly, monthly, quarterly and yearly), and also have a plan in place for dealing with unexpected expenses. Additionally, you should have enough savings or a line of credit to cover unexpected expenses, such as equipment breakdowns, a drop in sales, fire, flood, pestilence, COVID... you get my drift.

It is also important for you as a small business owner to seek professional advice from a financial advisor and/or accountant, who will help you develop and implement a financial plan for you personally and for your business. This will help you make informed decisions about how to manage your finances and your business finances, and can also help you identify future problems before they become too serious. For example, a financial advisor can help a small business owner set a budget and a cash flow projection, which may identify developing problems before they occur. At Ceebeks, we help business owners with a business and financial plan so that they understand their tax obligations, and we help them take advantage of tax deductions and credits.

Chasers Tip

Financial instability is a real concern for small businesses, but it can be avoided with proper planning and management. By keeping accurate records, planning a budget, and seeking professional advice, small business owners can ensure that their business stays financially stable and continues to grow. Being aware of the warning signs of financial instability such as not being able to pay bills on time, a large amount of debt or a significant drop in sale, allows business owners to take steps to prevent financial instability before it becomes a problem.

3. Lack of customers - A small business needs customers to survive. Without them, it will fail

In 2015, we heard about cloud-based systems and how a paperless office could be achieved to help play our role in reducing waste and the number of trees required to supply paper.

This set our business on the path of being totally online.

To do this, we really focused on who our ideal customers were, what they wanted, how we could best help them resolve their problems and needs, and the most efficient way we could provide our services to them. Understanding our target audience allowed us to design and build our business in readiness for the new digital landscape we would be operating from in the future.

We researched and began using the Google suite of products for our internal processes, cloud-based accounting software – Xero for our accounting processes - online appointment setting apps, and a dynamic website that adopted the AIDA Model (Attention, Interest, Desire, Action) or 'marketing funnel' as it is more commonly known. We offered meetings online, which enabled us to better service our remote customers and expand our 'reach' across the country, and we expanded our Team to include several international team members due to the shortage of experts in Australia.

Little did we know that the world would be virtually shut down in 2020 during the global pandemic, but we were perfectly placed to deal with it as our Team was able to seamlessly deliver the valuable support services our customers needed to survive.

When it comes to online marketing and lead generation, businesses face the challenge of deciding which social media platforms or advertising channels to use among the multitude of options available.

Furthermore, the digital landscape is constantly evolving.

Here are some considerations and strategies to navigate this challenge:

- **Defining Goals and Target Audience:** Start by clearly defining your marketing goals and identifying your target audience. Understanding your target audience's demographics, interests, and online behaviour will help you determine the most suitable social media platforms and advertising channels to reach them.

- **Research and Analysis:** Conduct research to identify the platforms that align with your target audience and industry. Analyse the demographics, user engagement, and advertising options available on each platform to make informed decisions.
- **Test and Optimise:** Rather than spreading your resources thin across multiple platforms, begin with a few key platforms that are most likely to yield results. Launch campaigns and track their performance using analytics tools. Continuously optimise your campaigns based on the data you collect to improve their efficacy.
- **Cost-Effective Strategies:** To maximise your budget, consider outsourcing certain tasks to a virtual team in countries like the Philippines, where labour is readily available, the people are eager to work, and costs may be lower. This could include content creation, social media management, or customer support. However, you will need to ensure active communication and management to maintain quality and consistency in delivery.
- **Website Optimisation:** Invest in developing a good website with a user-friendly interface. Optimise it for search engines (SEO) to improve organic traffic. Implement a seamless checkout process for e-commerce, enabling easy browsing, product selection, and ordering. Prioritise user experience and ensure mobile responsiveness.
- **Lead Generation Funnels:** Implement lead generation funnels to capture and nurture possible customers. Create compelling

and valuable content offers such as eBooks, webinars or free trials to attract leads. Use landing pages, email marketing, and automated workflows to guide leads through the sales funnel.

- **Google Reviews and Online Reputation:** Encourage satisfied customers to leave positive reviews on Google and other relevant review platforms. Monitor and respond to customer reviews promptly to build trust and credibility. Having a system that automates process is a time-saver!
- **Digital Magazines:** like our National Award-Winning **Chasing The Dream Magazine** on the **Mobimag Platform**, provide an interactive and engaging platform to showcase your brand, industry expertise, and valuable content. Here's how they can help attract new customers:

   a. **Content Promotion:** Digital magazines allow you to create and distribute prime content to a targeted audience. By publishing informative articles, interviews, case studies, and industry insights, you can position yourself as a thought leader and attract likely customers who are seeking rélevant information.

   b. **Brand Visibility:** Being featured in digital magazines can increase your brand's visibility and exposure. It provides an opportunity to reach a wider audience and capture the attention of individuals who might not otherwise be aware of your business.

   c. **Networking and Partnerships:** Digital magazines often collaborate with industry influencers, experts, and businesses. By contributing to or being featured in these magazines, you can establish connections and partnerships that may lead to new customer acquisition opportunities.

d. **Lead Generation:** Digital magazines often allow you to include calls-to-action, links or advertisements within your content. This can drive traffic to your website or landing pages, generating leads and potential customers who are interested in your offerings.

- **Podcasts:** have gained significant popularity, and provide a unique avenue for reaching and engaging with prospective customers. Our new podcast, The Chasers Channel, available on Spotify and other podcast hosting platforms, contributes to our customer acquisition strategy by:

    a. Thought Leadership: Hosting a podcast allows you to share your expertise, insights, and industry knowledge with your target audience. By delivering valuable and informative content, you can establish yourself as an authority in your field, attracting listeners who are interested in your professionalism, and perhaps converting them into customers.

    b. Audience Expansion: Podcasts offer the opportunity to tap into new audiences that may not engage with other forms of content. Listeners often subscribe to podcasts based on their interests or specific topics, providing you with access to a targeted and engaged audience.

c. Guest Collaborations: Inviting industry experts, influencers or customers as guests on your podcast can create collaborations and cross-promotion opportunities. This allows you to leverage their audience and reach, attracting new listeners who may become customers.

d. Call-to-Action and Engagement: Within podcast episodes, you can include call-to-action messages to encourage listeners to visit your website, sign up for newsletters or engage with your brand on social media. This can drive traffic and generate leads, leading to customer acquisition.

To maximise the impact of your strategies, ensure that your content is valuable, engaging, and tailored to your target audience. Consistency, quality, and promotion are key to attracting and retaining listeners and readers. Leverage social media, email marketing, and partnerships to amplify the reach of your digital magazine or podcast, and attract new customers.

Remember, online marketing and lead generation require ongoing efforts – they are not something that you do once and then forget about. Set realistic timeframes, and expect small, incremental improvements as you gather data and refine your strategies. Stay updated with the latest industry trends, and adapt your approach accordingly – AI and the use of these new tools is the next technological revolution, and you need to be part of it or risk getting left behind!

Customers are the life blood of any business - all businesses need customers to survive. Without customers, a business will not make any money and will not be able to pay its bills. This can lead to it going bankrupt and having to close.

Partnerships, joint ventures, and sponsorships can indeed be valuable sources of new customers, and actively assist marketing efforts. Here's how these collaborations can benefit your business:

1. **Partnerships and Joint Ventures:** Collaborating with complementary businesses, which your business is not directly competing with, or industry leaders, can help you tap into their existing customer base and expand your reach. By combining resources, expertise, and audiences, you can create mutually beneficial campaigns, co-branded products or joint events that attract new customers - at a fraction of the cost of going it alone!
2. **Sponsorships:** Sponsoring events, conferences or community initiatives relevant to your target audience can raise brand visibility and generate leads. Choose sponsorships that align with your brand values and target demographic to maximise the impact. Use the sponsorship to engage with attendees, showcase your products/services, and capture prospective customers' attention.
3. **Influencer Marketing:** The rise of influencers has transformed content marketing by leveraging individuals with large online followings to promote products or services. Influencers have

built trust and credibility with their audience, supporting their recommendations. People like Julie Goodwin of Master Chef fame and Adam Gilchrist from Australia Test Cricket are a couple of celebrity examples of influencers who promote products. Partnering with influencers who resonate with your target audience can help increase brand awareness, drive traffic, and generate leads. Check out https://pickstar.pro if you want to get started.

Incorporating influencers into your content marketing strategy can provide the following benefits:

a. **Expanded Reach:** Influencers have a dedicated following that trusts their opinions and recommendations. When an influencer promotes your brand, they expose your business to their audience, perhaps reaching new customers.

b. **Authenticity and Trust:** Influencers are seen as authentic voices in their respective niches. When they endorse your products or services, it carries a level of trust that traditional advertising may lack. This can positively impact the perception of your brand and increase customer engagement.

c. **Diversified Content:** Collaborating with influencers allows you to diversify your content by leveraging their creativity and unique perspectives. This variety can help keep your content fresh and engaging, and appeal to a wider audience.

d. **Social Proof:** Influencer endorsements can provide social proof, demonstrating to potential customers that your products or services are valued and endorsed by someone they trust.

When working with influencers, ensure that they align with your brand values and have an engaged and relevant audience. Establish clear goals, expectations, and metrics for measuring the success of influencer campaigns.

As you're a small business, you don't have unlimited time or money to invest in marketing and advertising so you need to formulate a Marketing Plan and then execute it. A good Marketing Plan will contain some or all the following:

- **Business Purpose** - which describes your objective for the business
- **Competitive Advantage** - the main points of difference in your market
- **Business Goals** - the top areas of focus for the next 12 months
- **Marketing Goals** - how many new customers you need to achieve those goals
- **Target Market** - who your ideal customer is - their demographics & psychographics
- **Capture Strategy** - the main ways you will capture leads
- **Nurture Strategy** - the main ways you will care for and support your leads

- **Conversion Strategy** - the main ways you convert your leads into customers
- **Optimisation Strategy** - the main ways you increase sales to current customers
- **Reactivation Strategy** - the main ways you re-engage with past customers
- **Marketing Campaign** - define the strategy, who is responsible and who can help, and what its success looks like
- **Action Steps** - the five main steps to implement this campaign
- **Campaign Summary** - how you measure the success of the campaign
- **Results Tracker** - record the prospects targeted, leads generated, cost per lead, sales generated, average cost of sales, and how many customers you have retained or lost
- **Learnings** - the things you have learnt from completing this Marketing Plan
- **Roadblocks** - the things that will hold you back from achieving these goals
- **Next Steps** - a list of the immediate next steps to start implementing your new Marketing Plan.

A link to The Simplest Marketing Plan template for you to use is provided in the Appendices at the end of this book.

A critical part of your marketing is to fully understand your customer, and you need to undertake some research to do this. Don't assume you know your customer or that people who have worked with you before (perhaps in someone else's business) will follow you to your own business.

You must understand what your customer wants/needs, when they want it (their challenges), how they currently go about researching where to get it, and what price they are willing to pay. 'Open it and they will come' is not a business strategy or a Marketing Plan.

In 2023 online marketing is a vital part of any Marketing Plan, and it's the area that can suck up large sums of money and time for vague results unless you know what you're doing. There are thousands of offerings out there in the online world for lead generation funnels that promise to make you millions (guess what - most don't work), and the people spruiking these are the ones making millions. You can spend tens of thousands of dollars on funnels, Google Ads, Facebook Ads, LinkedIn Ads...ads, ads, ads, and content.

But if you're new to this world, don't get sucked in!

Find a reputable adviser to guide you, and start small so you can learn as you go, and not break the bank.

Pricing your products or services is a critical aspect of your business strategy that can significantly impact your marketing efforts and customer acquisition. But beware of using discounting to 'get a foot in the door' to establish market share. Consistent discounting may be a good acquisition strategy and possibly even a good retention strategy, but when brands overuse the tool, customers begin to expect to only pay sale prices.

Consumers have been so desensitised to brightly coloured sale signs that what was once a useful tool to attract, retain, and upsell customers has become counterproductive. If an item isn't on sale, they will wait or go online to find a better price. Because thousands of retailers are running sales every hour of every day, consumers don't feel the need to capitalise immediately when they see one, and yet they still expect never to pay full price.

Here are some considerations for pricing your goods effectively:

1. **Value-Based Pricing:** Focus on the value your product or service provides to customers rather than solely considering costs or competition. Understand your target audience's pain points, needs, and desires, and price your offerings based on the value they perceive. Emphasise the benefits and unique selling propositions that differentiate you from competitors.

2. **Market Research:** Conduct thorough market research to gain insights into pricing trends, customer expectations, and competitor strategies. Analyse pricing models in your industry and evaluate where your offering fits within the market. Consider factors such as target market segment, product positioning, and perceived quality when setting your prices.

3. **Cost Analysis:** While value-based pricing is essential, it's also crucial to consider your costs to ensure profitability. Work out your production or service delivery costs, overhead expenses, and desired profit margins. Factor in variable costs such as materials and labour as well as fixed costs such as rent and equipment. Ensure that your pricing strategy covers these costs while still aligning with the perceived value of your offering. If you know your break-even cost and the number of sales you need to make each day, those are the key figures you must obsess over. One of my favourite marketing gurus Seth Godin suggests that you start with the minimum number of your ideal customers that can deliver a profit, and then start focusing on systems and scaling up from there - this is a great concept to grasp.
4. **Pricing Strategies:** Several pricing strategies can be used, depending on your business model and market dynamics. These include:

    a. Cost-Plus Pricing: Set a price by adding a markup percentage to your production costs

    b. Competitive Pricing: Price your offerings based on competitor prices, either matching, undercutting or positioning as a premium option

    c. Value-Based Pricing: Price based on the unique value your offering provides, focusing on customer benefits and differentiation

- d. Bundling or Upselling: Offer packages or add-on options to provide additional value to customers and justify steeper prices
- e. Psychological Pricing: Use pricing tactics such as charm pricing ($9.99 instead of $10) or tiered pricing (basic, standard, premium) to influence customer perception.

5. Pricing Flexibility: Consider offering different pricing tiers or options to cater to various customer segments or purchasing behaviours. This flexibility can accommodate different budgets or needs, attract a wider range of customers, and increase sales opportunities.
6. **Test and Adjust:** Pricing is not set in stone. I remember a very important quote from Paul Dunn way back when I attended The Accountants Boot Camp that he ran in 1999. 'to assume you know the price someone is willing to pay is ignorance in the extreme.' Not only that, if you provide enough value, they may pay more because the product or service is so important to them. Continuously monitor market dynamics, customer feedback, and performance metrics to evaluate the effectiveness of your pricing strategy. Conduct pricing experiments or A/B tests to determine optimal price points and adjust incrementally.

Remember, pricing decisions should align with your overall business objectives and brand positioning. Evaluate your pricing strategy regularly to ensure it remains competitive, profitable, and in line with customer expectations. Above all, offer more value than your competition and you will build customer loyalty.

Jim's Pastries

Jim's Pastries is a small bakery that makes delicious cakes and pastries. If no one comes to the bakery to buy the cakes and pastries, Jim's Pastries will not make any money. Without money, the bakery will not be able to pay its bills for things like rent, electricity, and ingredients. If this continues for too long, the bakery will have to close down.

> Our Solutions - identifying target customers, understanding their needs, and developing a marketing strategy to attract them

It's important to note that a lack of customers can happen for many reasons. Maybe the bakery or store is in a bad location where not many people go. Maybe there is too much competition in the area. Maybe the prices are too high. Whatever the reason, a small business needs to find ways to attract customers if it wants to survive, and taking the time to set out a Marketing Plan is the key.

In its early days, Jim's Pastries was struggling to get its name out there, and reached out to Ceebeks for help in developing a Marketing Plan. By creating brand awareness - offering tasting samples and specially packaged pastries in gift boxes - we were able to set Jim's Pastries apart from their competition to the extent that you now have to order in advance so as not to miss out.

Attracting customers

One way a business can attract customers is by having a sale or offering a special deal. For example, Jim's Pastries could offer a 'buy one get one free' deal on cakes. This might attract more customers who want to save money. Or a clothing store could have a clearance sale to move old stock. This might attract customers looking for a good deal.

Another way a business can attract customers is by advertising. Jim's Pastries put up signs in the neighbourhood, and advertised on social media with images of its mouthwatering creations, and even videos of customers enjoying them. This let people know where the bakery was and what it had to offer.

> **Chasers Tip**
>
> - Find ways to attract customers - best solved by creating a detailed Marketing Plan.
> - Research best practice websites and use a developer who delivers these.
> - Engage an experienced business coach.

4. Intense competition - Small businesses face ruthless competition from other businesses

You might have a great product or service for which there is steady demand, but your business could still fail.

Strong demand will eventually translate to a lot of competition, and therefore some businesses will fail to stand out in the crowd (Storey, 2016). Having an excellent product will not always be enough given the current trends and dynamics in the market, nor will offering excellent service to customers.

You always need to develop and nurture a unique value proposition, so you don't get lost among the competition.

And it's not a set-and-forget approach. With the economy and marketplace evolving constantly and social media companies changing their policies and algorithms, you need follow your marketing plan AND remain somewhat flexible in implementing it. Reviewing your data analytics or having someone on your Team who does is a must.

What sets your business apart from the competition?

What makes your business operations or service delivery unique?

As the business owner, you should always think and operate with these and other questions in mind.

It's never healthy practice to obsess over the competitors - however, you shouldn't ignore them either. When a competitor launches a similar product or service, you should know it inside out and be able to explain why you are better. It is essential that you understand what the competitors do better or differently, and whether this impacts on your offering, how, and to what extent. If you fail to differentiate, you can't build a dynamic, sustainable brand.

One thing that you can almost guarantee in business is that, if you are successful, it won't take long before someone else comes along and tries to copy what you have done.

Small businesses often face intense competition. This means many other businesses that offer similar products or services in the same area. This competition can make it difficult for a small business to survive.

Karli's Kaffeehaus

Karli's Kaffeehaus is a small coffee shop that serves the most amazing freshly ground coffee - the aroma hits you up the street as you walk towards them - and pastries. The coffee shop faced fierce competition from other franchised coffee shops in the area, which initially made it difficult for them to attract customers because there were already so many other places for people to have coffee, and the larger franchised shops had brand awareness.

Intense competition can make it difficult for a small business to survive, because it is hard to make a profit. If customers choose to shop elsewhere, the small business will not make enough money. Without enough money, it will not be able to pay its bills and may go bankrupt.

So what did they do and what happened - and how long did it take – and how did they fund the business while they were building it?

Our Solutions - differentiating the business, understanding the competition, and continually improving the business

To survive in an environment of cut-throat competition, small businesses can try to differentiate themselves by offering something unique or different.

Karli's Kaffeehaus changed the spelling of coffee house to reflect the owners' German heritage, and offered a special blend of coffee that couldn't be found anywhere else, and a wider selection of pastries.

They also found a way of dispersing the aroma of their special brand of coffee outside their shop so that any coffee lover passing by was instantly attracted.

A radio campaign describing 'the rich drops of lusciousness extracted from each sustainably sourced coffee bean which delivered the aroma that awakened the senses' drew an immediate response from coffee lovers everywhere with two weeks of airplay. Two new baristas were hired just to cover the peak service periods in the early morning, and at lunchtime and school pickup.

Another way for small businesses to survive intense competition is to focus on excellent customer service, which makes customers feel valued and appreciated. This can help to create a loyal customer base that will continue to shop there even in the face of fierce competition.

Chasers Tip

- Keeping your costs low. By keeping down costs, a small business can offer products or services at a lower price than the competition. This can make a small business more appealing to customers looking for a good deal.
- A proper understanding and analysis of your strengths and weaknesses, and those of your competitors, is crucial to withstand stiff competition from other businesses threatening your survival. A Marketing Plan helps to uncover these so that you can develop your USP (Unique Selling Position) to differentiate your business by offering something unique or different. By doing so, small businesses can attract customers and make good profits despite the competition.

5. Poor mindset - Poor management can lead to a lack of direction and a lack of control over the business

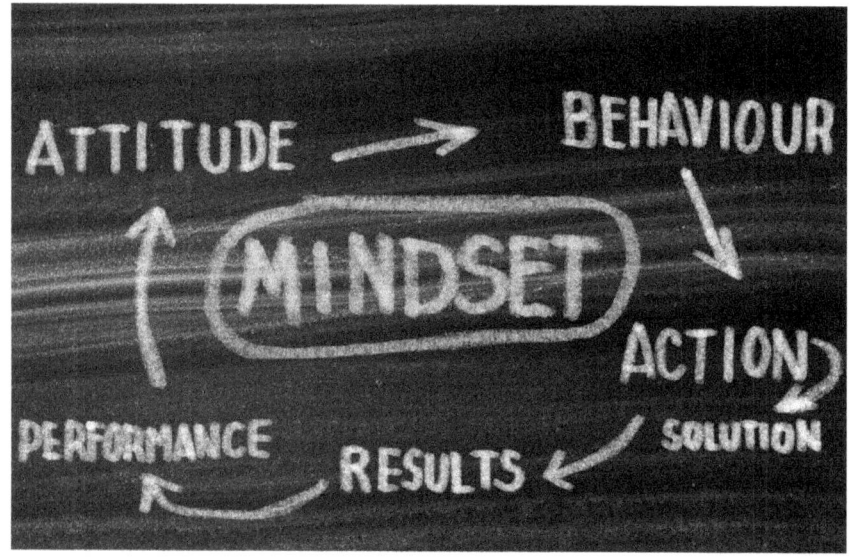

In an Australian Centre for Business Growth study, the most common dominant factor in the many reasons why businesses fail is the inability of management to understand their roles and responsibilities as the heads of small business entities. Managers need to plan and set the company's direction, communicate, build an executive team, create a high-performance culture of execution, and manage and optimise corporate resources – including employees and financial resources, customers, suppliers, vendors, advisors, and financiers (Burns & Dewhurst, 2016). It is not the plan that is crucial: it is the planning.

Poor management is another core reason for failure. Leaders need to understand their responsibilities and role as organisation leader (DIISR&TE., 2012). While larger companies can manage a short while without leadership in place, small businesses cannot. The dynamics between a small number of employees/contractors can quickly turn sour without the containing presence of a strong leader. The leader's primary role lies in defining the business strategy. They need to put in place good governance and a culture of learning, and ensure that all operations consistently point in that precise direction.

Unforeseen futures

It's easy to plan for growth, however often what is missed is preparing for an unforeseen future. Every business exists in a world with extraneous factors full of unpredictable dynamics like politics, interest rates, climate change, and global trends. Most small business managers do not take such elements into account (Longenecker et al., 2013), and this indicates a downward spiral for many promising SMEs. Once the worst happens, what will you do about it? The way you choose to respond is crucial. In 2016, for instance, Toyota CEO Jim Lentz handled its PR crisis himself when several million cars were suddenly recalled — personally coming out to help the situation by answering questions online and on social media platforms. Had he waited for the chain of command, what might have happened?

Business enterprises fail because of the lack of both short- and long-term planning. Most leaders have no clear strategy, and get caught up in the day-to-day of what the business requires, but pay little attention to long-term plans (Colombo et al., p.183, 2012), hence failing to improve on the business operations or the strategic approach. This might be you. You started your business by working in it, and you may still be doing so. You're so busy doing – juggling, delivering, and securing new work/contracts/sales, and all the other aspects of running the business - that you don't have time to work 'on' your business. Working on your business is the planning part. And you need a Business Plan.

Your Business Plan should include where your business will be in the next few months to the next few years. Include measurable goals and results, and track them weekly at least - even if you're only tracking yourself.

If you are merely working in the business, you need to spend time working on it. Allocate regular time for strategic and business planning (Kotey, p.356, 2017).

The right plan should have specific to-do lists with dates and deadlines. Failure to plan will damage your business. Hope is not a plan; it's waiting for someone else to take action, and that rarely ends well for small businesses.

Businesses fail because of poor leadership

As the business owner, you're the leader. As the leader you must be able to stand your ground and make sound decisions most of the time - right from financial matters to those involving contractors, employees, suppliers, and partners.

Leadership failures will affect every aspect of your business operations. Examples of poor leadership and management cover the inability to listen, micromanaging, lack of trust, working without standards or systems, poor communication, and lack of feedback. In such cases, when problems requiring outstanding leadership arise, you may be reluctant to take charge and resolve the issues while the business continues to slip towards failure. Without strategic and business planning, business success and growth is accidental, and while your company might have great promise, it may equally fail.

I highlighted the phrase 'entrepreneurial seizure' earlier as a reason why some people start a business - where they were the expert in the technical work of the business they were employed in, and thought that because they knew that, they were qualified to run the business.

Well, without leadership and management skills to run a business this is fraught with danger, and another major reason why businesses fail.

If you haven't had any management or leadership training, or taken any personal development programs, I recommend that you consider this before or as you are building your business: leadership is not innate and can be learnt. And, you must learn it if you are going to build a successful small business. Even if it's learning skills of self-leadership and awareness, your business will benefit.

Engaging a business coach, enrolling in self-paced leadership courses, and joining business groups that encourage and develop leadership skills are critical if you are employing people and want to develop a team that can take you to your dream business destination.

The right mindset

Part of leadership is having the right mindset.

So what is the 'right' mindset?

In today's fast-paced and ever-evolving business landscape, visionary leadership plays a pivotal role in driving success and fostering growth within the Team. While leadership skills can be honed through experience and education, one decisive factor that sets exceptional leaders apart is their mindset. A leader's mindset encompasses their beliefs, attitude, and perspective, shaping their approach to problem-solving, decision-making, and team management.

At a recent conference, I attended a masterclass by Joe Pane on Emotional Fitness - and identifying the five core principles that significantly impact our capacity to handle life's challenges. Having an awareness of who you are, the stage of life you are at, and clarity in what matters most in your life, a healthy emotional vocabulary, and clean perspective are what it means to be emotionally fit.

The key elements I learnt about having the right mindset that empowers leaders to navigate the challenges of leading a Business Team successfully were:

1. Growth Orientation:

Leaders with the right mindset understand the value of continuous personal and professional growth. They embrace this growth-oriented mindset, recognising that their skills and abilities can be developed through effort, learning, and experience. This perspective encourages leaders to seek out opportunities for self-improvement, take calculated risks, and promote a culture of learning within their Team. By having a growth mindset, leaders inspire their Team Members to push boundaries, innovate, and continuously improve their skills, actually driving the overall success of the business.

2. Visionary Thinking:

Effective leaders possess a visionary mindset, capable of imagining a future state and charting a clear path to achieve it. They have the ability to see beyond the immediate challenges, and picture the potential of their Team and the organisation. A visionary mindset allows leaders to communicate a compelling vision, inspire others to share in that vision, and align Team efforts towards common goals. By painting a vivid picture of success and providing a sense of purpose, leaders can motivate and engage their Team Members, fostering a collective commitment to achieving extraordinary results.

3. Emotional Intelligence:

The right mindset for leadership encompasses emotional intelligence: the ability to understand and manage your own emotions and relate successfully to others. Leaders with emotional intelligence are empathetic, self-aware, and skilled at building positive relationships. They create an environment of trust, where Team Members feel valued and supported, enabling open communication and collaboration. By demonstrating emotional intelligence, leaders can resolve conflicts, provide constructive feedback, and inspire their team to perform at their best, driving productivity, and fostering a harmonious work culture.

4. Adaptability and Resilience:

In today's dynamic business environment, change is inevitable. Leaders with the right mindset embrace change as an opportunity for growth and innovation rather than a threat. They are adaptable and resilient, which allow them to navigate uncertainty, overcome obstacles, and inspire their team to do the same. By remaining flexible and open to new ideas, leaders can make informed decisions, adapt strategies, and lead their Team through turbulent times. Their resilience helps them bounce back from setbacks, learn from failures, and motivate their Team to persevere in the face of adversity.

The right mindset is a fundamental aspect of outstanding leadership in the business world. Leaders with the right mindset embrace growth, think strategically, and display emotional intelligence. By cultivating these qualities, leaders inspire their Team Members, drive innovation, and create a positive and productive work environment. It is through the power of the right mindset that leaders navigate the complexities of guiding a business team, overcome challenges, and achieve remarkable success.

Conversely, a poor mindset may lead to a number of negative outcomes that can harm your business and eventually cause it to fail. Some characteristics of a poor mindset are:

- **Negative attitude:** Do you know of or have you met someone who is constantly complaining, whinging, swears at customers who complain or just has a bad attitude about everything, and yet they run a business? A negative attitude can spread throughout an organisation and impact morale, motivation and productivity. For example, if you consistently focus on the negative aspects of your business and discourage your employees, this can lead to poor morale and motivation among the staff, contractors, suppliers, and partners.
- **Lack of vision:** A lack of vision can prevent a business from moving forward and reaching its full potential. For example, if

you lack a clear vision for the future, you may not be able to set goals convincingly or make decisions that will benefit the company in the long term.

- **Resistance to change:** 'We've always done it this way and we're not changing now!' I had a boss like this many years ago - very set in his ways and forceful in his ideas. Resistance to change can prevent a business from adapting to new challenges and opportunities. Xero cloud accounting is a great example of how business owners who embraced new technologies or ideas were able to take on opportunities for growth and improvement by outsourcing their accounting work.
- **Failure to embrace failure:** 'Let the fear of failure be the background noise of your success.' — Giovanni Dienstmann. Failing to embrace failure as a learning opportunity can prevent a business (and you) from learning from your mistakes and improving. For example, if the owner of the plumbing business constantly blames his young apprentices for mistakes instead of finding out the root cause of the problem, they will not be able to make the necessary changes to improve their operations. Quite often, it is the instruction process that breaks down, and this can easily be solved by developing systems and processes for employees to follow.
- **Failure to seek help:** Running a business involves wearing several hats, and quite often failing to seek help when needed can prevent a business from making risky decisions or the necessary changes to improve and grow. For example, if a

business owner chooses not to seek the advice of experts or hire consultants, they may miss out on valuable insights that could improve their operations. This is especially so when the business is facing financial pressure.

A poor mindset can be a major barrier to success. It is important for you to cultivate a positive and growth-oriented mindset, embrace failure as a learning opportunity, and seek help when needed to succeed in today's competitive business environment.

Poor management can threaten the survival of a business. When management is inefficient, it can lead to a lack of direction and a lack of control, which can cause several problems, including low productivity, low and declining morale among employees, and lower profits.

Coastal Butchers

Coastal Butchers was a classic example of poor management. The manager was a technician when it came to the butchery skills - he could cut up a carcass perfectly in no time - but he did not set clear goals or expectations for his Team. Without clear goals, his Team constantly waited for instructions, would be on their mobile phones throughout the day, and left early without taking proper cleaning and safety measures. They simply did not know what was expected of them, and were not motivated to work towards any goals. This led to decreased productivity and a lack of focus on tasks that needed to be completed, such as fat being left on the floor that caused accidents, wastage of product, constant tension between the manager and Team as to who should be doing what, and the manager taking on extra work to complete tasks other people should have done.

When they came to Ceebeks a year before COVID, it was too late to help them navigate a way back to survival as the last remaining member of their Team could no longer fill orders and meet their ongoing commitments. Unfortunately, the arrival of COVID was really a blessing for the business, and it was shut down.

> **Our Solutions include setting clear goals, creating a plan to achieve them, and regularly reviewing progress**

Poor management can also lead to a lack of control. When a manager is not in control, they may not be able to make important decisions or take the necessary action to keep things running smoothly. This can lead to financial losses, and eventually the business may not survive.

In order to avoid these problems, it is important for managers to provide clear goals and expectations for employees, adequate support and resources, and to maintain control over the business. By doing so, they can help ensure the survival of the business.

Chasers Tip

- Poor management not only affects the employees but also the customers. Unhappy employees can lead to unhappy customers and that can lead to loss of customers, which in turn affects the business revenues.
- Regular Team meetings at the start and end of the week as minimum are a great way of keeping the whole Team focused on individual goals set for the week and accountability in achieving them. Regular meetings also help keep up morale and show that management cares about each Team Member's well-being.
- Team social events are another great way of showing interest and care, and keeping up morale.

NOTE: If you are operating your business with a virtual team or a combination of virtual, work-from-home, and office members, it is even more important to bring the whole Team together virtually, so that everyone is engaged and feels supported.

6. Unexpected legal or regulatory issues - Small businesses can be blindsided by unexpected legal or regulatory issues

Entrepreneurs cannot control external or macroeconomic factors used by governments at regional, national or global levels, such as raising interest rates, taxes or government spending to regulate the economy's growth and stability. Then there are common external factors such as business cycles, calamities like fire, drought, recession, war, global trends, natural disasters, government debt, inflation, COVID, and changes in policy (Lignier & Evans, 2012). Failure to anticipate such events, not having contingency plans in place in time or even failing to consult the right professionals such as lawyers or your accountant or financial adviser means that your business might not withstand the storm. I have heard countless stories from business owners about how the GFC in 2008-09 and then COVID in 2020-22 wiped out their businesses. Some were forced into administration and/or liquidation, with the owners having to sell their homes and more.

A small business can still succeed in bad times IF you act soon enough and the correct and appropriate measures are taken in time.

Unexpected legal or regulatory issues can also have a profound impact on the survival of a small business. These issues come in many forms, and can blindside you as the owner, leaving you unprepared and causing financial losses.

In 2000, the Federal Government introduced a new tax system, GST, which imposed additional compliance costs ranging from $3,331 to $30,140 on many businesses according to research by the Small Business Research Unit at Victorian University, where two of the smallest businesses reviewed said their compliance costs amounted to over 3% of their reported annual turnover. Furthermore, managing the changes that this new tax system brought was another problem as many businesses who were just surviving had failed to set aside the GST they collected from their customers to pass on to the ATO when they reported on their Business Activity Statement. They did not appreciate that they were 'pseudo-tax collectors' and spent this windfall that came into their bank accounts. Many were then unable to meet their tax obligations, and so their businesses were closed down as a consequence of ATO collection enforcement or voluntary cessation.

Another more recent example of unexpected regulatory issues was the COVID pandemic, which resulted in Government regulations to lock down States and Regions in an attempt to curtail the spread of the virus. According to a Small Business Australia survey conducted by the Australian Bureau of Statistics, 10% of the 220,000 businesses questioned indicated they would close after government financial support ended. Many were forced into insolvency and bankruptcy caused by the public health crisis response, this despite various government support packages such as JobKeeper and small business grants.

The lockdowns were extremely hard on businesses as they had no choice in the matter. However, those that sought advice and support on whether they qualified for federal and state grants, JobKeeper and other support, were in a much better position, maintaining operations through the pandemic and then restarting when the bulk of the restrictions were lifted.

Stevo's Security Service

Stevo's was in demand: they had a high turnover, a large number of customers who regularly paid on time, reasonably good staff, and an accounting system that was in good shape.

However, the owners did not account for the GST paid to them by their customers, and failed to set this aside for payment to the ATO. Nor did they set aside the PAYG (Pay as You Go) Tax on their employees' wages nor the SGC (Superannuation Guarantee Charge). The 'extra' money in the bank after paying the general costs was drawn out, and used to fund their lifestyles.

It wasn't very long before the ATO was owed thousands of dollars; their employees lodged complaints about the superannuation deficiencies in their member accounts, and audits were undertaken by the Fair Work Commission.

Unfortunately, when Stevo's came to us for help, they were in far too much debt, and all we could do was to assist them to liquidate and wind up the business.

Two important issues to know about when placing a company into administration or liquidation are:

1. Once an administrator/liquidator is appointed, you CANNOT make ANY decisions about your business. You are legally required to work with the administrator throughout the process, which can take a lot of your time for little or no payment, and you don't have access to your business bank accounts.
2. As a director of a company that has gone into administration, this will have a serious effect on your ability to secure finance in the future as you will have to declare this on any loan or finance application. Many banks will simply not lend you money, forcing you to deal with non-bank or low doc lenders, which charge higher rates of interest.

Our Solutions - stay informed about relevant laws and regulations, and seek legal advice when necessary

Unexpected regulatory issues may also arise. For example, a business may be unaware of a certain safety standard, new compliance, insurance or registration requirements and, as a result, forced to close down or pay penalties.

To avoid such issues, you need to stay informed about legal and regulatory changes that could affect your operations. You should also consult legal and regulatory experts to ensure you are in compliance with all applicable laws and regulations. Not knowing is not a defence.

Chasers Tip

- Get professional legal, financial and accounting advice when you don't understand new laws and regulations. This will help guide you, and help your business navigate through legal issues.

7. Burnout - Small business owners often wear many hats and have to handle various tasks, leading to burnout

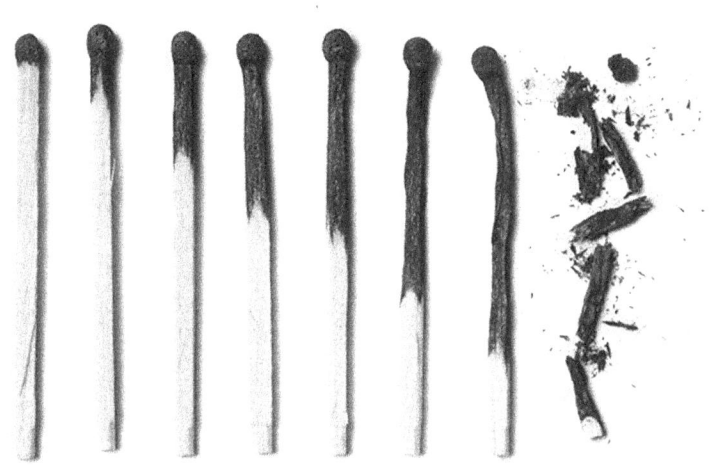

Running a business involves managing cash flow, chasing up overdue debtors, answering the phone, making appointments, instructing, leading and managing Team Members, scheduling work, doing the work, sending out invoices, preparing marketing campaigns, etc.

And in many cases, including mine in the very early days, it involved the business owner performing ALL of these roles on their own.

In the words of Michael Gerber – they're 'doing it, doing it, doing it!'

And eventually it takes a toll, in the form of burnout.

Burnout is a common issue for small business owners, who must often wear many hats and handle many tasks. This can lead to feelings of exhaustion, cynicism, and not getting things done. Burnout can have a huge impact on the survival of a business, as it can lead to less productivity and poor decision-making. It can also affect your relationships and family. Remember that desire to work for yourself to achieve a better work-life balance? For many, it becomes the work nightmare where there's no balance and you feel you're on a running wheel.

Eric's Electrical

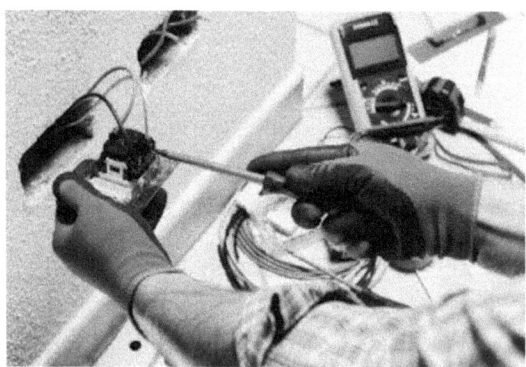

Eric's Electrical is a typical example of burnout shaping a business.

Eric had the idea of servicing the neighbourhood with pick-up and drop-off electrical repairs. This was in complete contrast to other repairers who required a drop-off and sent the appliance away to the manufacturer's preferred repairer. The problem was that Eric was the only person in the business, so he had to schedule times to collect the goods, bring them back to his workshop, order parts, organise the work, do it, arrange a delivery time with the customer, prepare the invoice, collect payment, and manage his marketing.

It didn't take very long before he realised he was in trouble. He was increasingly stressed and exhausted, and began to neglect important tasks such as ordering new inventory and managing the store's finances. He couldn't deal with any new business or even meet the demands of existing customers because he couldn't cope. This led to lower sales volume and cash flow, which ultimately resulted in having to shut down the business and walk away.

> **Our Solutions - setting boundaries, delegating tasks, and taking time off when necessary**

In this example, the small business owner has become overwhelmed by their many responsibilities, which have led to burnout. This burnout then destroyed the business through decreased productivity and poor decision-making, ending in closure, the loss of the investment, and a struggle to meet remaining commitments to the landlord and other investors.

Chasers Tip

1. Recognise the signs of burnout and take steps to prevent it.
   Signs of burnout:
   - Trouble sleeping
   - Bad eating habits
   - Irritability with customers, family and friends
   - Substance abuse - alcohol, drugs
   - Missing out on important family events
   - Feeling overwhelmed – never getting on top of things
   - Fear of opening emails/letters from the ATO, ASIC, suppliers, your accountant.

2. Set boundaries - don't take work home - or set hours if working from home, then shut the door
3. Delegate tasks - and if you don't have someone to delegate to, find someone
4. Set clear hours for work, and schedule time off
5. Automate as much as you can - invoicing, payments, reporting – and use cloud-based software like Xero

6. Allocate time each week to specific tasks, and do these without being distracted
7. Get a business mentor or coach
8. Take time off to rest and recharge.

By addressing burnout, you can ensure your health and well-being, and the survival and success of your business.

8. No online presence - A strong online presence is crucial in today's market

Access to social media and internet services in Australia is quite easy. According to the ABS, in 2020 about 93% of households in Australia had internet access, and about 92% of individuals aged 18 years and over had used the Internet in the previous 12 months. They also reported that about 83% of individuals aged 18 years and over had a social media account.

Since such a large percentage of the Australian population has access to the Internet and social media, businesses in Australia have a large possible customer base to reach through online platforms.

It's worth noting that access to Internet and social media services may vary depending on the region, demographic, and income level. For example, households in urban areas may have better access than households in rural areas. Additionally, certain demographic groups such as the elderly may use the Internet and social media services less than younger groups. Certainly different age groups access different social media platforms . . . and it's up to you to work out which social media platforms your target customers use.

The percentage of businesses that have an online presence varies, depending on the region and industry. According to a National Small Business Association (NSBA) survey, in the United States 97% of small businesses have a website, and 86% of small businesses use social media for business purposes.

The percentage of Australian businesses with an online presence is quite high. The 2020 ABS survey reports that about 96% of Australian businesses have a website, and about 84% use social media for business purposes.

This shows that a vast majority of Australian businesses understand the importance of having an online presence, and use the Internet to reach customers and promote their products and services. Furthermore, businesses are also using online platforms such as Google and Yelp to generate customer reviews, which can increase trust and credibility.

Additionally, certain retail and service-based industries may have a higher percentage of businesses with an online presence than agriculture or construction.

However, it's worth noting that having a website or social media accounts is not enough. An active and engaging online presence is also important. Businesses should update their website and social media accounts regularly with relevant information, and engage with customers through online platforms to benefit from the potential customer base. How often you need to engage and with what content varies from platform to platform. TikTok is for short videos, Facebook for photos, videos, and text, Instagram for photos, short videos and posts, LinkedIn for longer posts, articles, videos, and more.

Having a constant online presence is crucial for the survival of any business. The Internet has become an integral part of our lives, and people use it to find products, services, and information. If a business doesn't have an online presence, it's missing out on a large potential customer base.

A key part of being online is being searchable, and the reviews that brings. Being searchable means you need to come up towards the top of the list in a Google search. You can achieve this through either 'organic' or paid content (advertising, influencers, etc.), but both require you to understand the basics of Search Engine Optimisation (SEO). The world of search is complicated and often costly, so it's important that you work with reputable people and learn the basics, and understand the investment in time and money you'll need to make as well as the return.

This goes for building or rebuilding your website. You can spend tens of thousands of dollars on a website, eCommerce, Customer Relationship Management system, photos, videos, landing pages, eBooks, and more, OR not. Understanding what you need and what you don't to promote your business online takes a lot of learning... as does finding the right partner, supplier and adviser to work with you.

A Taste of Spain Tapas Bar

A Taste of Spain Tapas Bar is a small local wine bar in a regional town that only has a physical store. They source hard to find exotic spirits, liquors and wines, but they don't have a website or social media accounts. Potential customers who are searching for their business online can't find them, and end up going to a competitor with a stronger online presence. This means that A Taste of Spain Tapas Bar is losing out on a lot of business.

> **Our Solutions – build a website, social media presence and online marketing strategies to be able to reach customers**

When we were in the initial discussions setting up the A Taste of Spain Tapas Bar website, we drafted the online presence strategy in their Marketing Plan, and introduced them to our national and global Expert in Website Strategy and Development, who created an amazing experience and solution for customers looking to buy their products.

By having a dynamic modern website, they are now able to maintain a compelling online presence, deliver personalised experiences, and fully engage with their target audience - lovers of exotic spirits, liquors and wines. They can now market directly to their online customers, and track their business performance and growth in the digital landscape.

After just three months, traffic to their physical store had increased by 27% in the middle of winter. In addition, regular patrons started ordering, and there were more national and international orders.

An online presence is not just about having a website though; it's also about using social media platforms such as Facebook, Twitter, Instagram, etc., to connect with customers and promote your business. For example, a retail store that posts pictures of new products, discounts, and events on social media can attract customers and boost sales. Businesses can use online platforms such as Google and Yelp to generate customer reviews, which may increase trust and credibility. If you're in the tourism sector you need to be on relevant aggregation sites such as AirBnB, Stayz, Booking.com as well as state and local tourism platforms.

Different industries and sectors have different platforms, and it's up to you to work out which ones are best for your business.

Chasers Tip

- Having a constant online presence is crucial for the survival of any business in today's market. It involves creating and keeping up to date both a website and social media accounts - and engaging with customers through online platforms can help attract new customers and increase sales.
- If you don't have an online presence, your business is missing out on a lot of possible business, and will be at a considerable disadvantage compared to your competitors.

9. Employee turnover - Rapid employee turnover can be detrimental to a small business

Rapid employee turnover can lead to lower productivity and profitability, and in some cases cause your business to fail. Some of the ways in which fast employee turnover can be detrimental to a small business:

1. **Increased Costs:** Hiring and training new employees is costly and time-consuming, especially for a small business with limited resources. The cost of recruiting, interviewing, and onboarding new employees, as well as the cost of lost productivity during the transition period, can add up quickly and strain the business's finances.

2. **Decreased Productivity:** Rapid employee turnover can disrupt the flow of work and lead to decreased productivity as new employees are trained and acclimate to their role. In addition, the departure of experienced employees can mean that the business loses the institutional knowledge and expertise that those employees brought to the job.
3. **Decreased Morale:** Rapid employee turnover can have a negative impact on the morale of remaining employees, leading to lower motivation and job satisfaction. This in turn can lead to decreased productivity and increased absenteeism, creating a vicious cycle that is difficult to break.
4. **Decreased Customer Satisfaction:** Rapid employee turnover can also upset customers. When clients interact with new employees who are not familiar with their company or its products, they may get subpar service, leading to a loss of trust in the business.
5. **Difficulty in Building a Strong Corporate Culture:** Rapid employee turnover can make it difficult for a small business to build a strong corporate culture, as new employees may not fully embrace the company's values and mission. This can lead to a lack of cohesion and direction, making it more difficult for the business to achieve its goals.

When all these negative impacts combine they will drag down a business and cause it to fail if not quickly addressed.

> Our Solutions - hiring the right people for the right roles, aligning everyone with the vision and goals of the business, creating a positive work environment, and offering competitive compensation and benefits

Someone who lacks motivation, is disinterested, or more interested in their social media account, will not be a suitable candidate for your customer service role.

Reducing employee turnover is essential for the success and sustainability of a small business. Ways that can help reduce employee turnover and retain valuable Team Members include:

- **Improving Workplace Culture:** A positive workplace culture can go a long way to retaining employees and reducing turnover. It can be achieved by creating a supportive and inclusive work environment, recognising and rewarding employee contributions, and fostering open and honest communication. Try a Team Retreat once a year to plan the upcoming year's objectives and targets, and hold smaller, shorter quarterly sessions too.
- **Offering Competitive Salary Packages and Benefits:** Offering competitive compensation and benefits packages can help attract and retain employees. These include not only competitive salaries, but also benefits such as health insurance, retirement plans, and paid time off, like 'Our Team enjoy a day off for their birthday to celebrate.'

- **Providing Professional Development Opportunities:** Providing opportunities for professional development and growth can make employees feel valued and motivated to stay with the company. These can include offering training and career advancement opportunities, as well as mentorship and coaching programs.
- **Improving Communication and Transparency:** Improving communication and transparency can help build trust and foster a positive workplace culture. This includes regular check-ins with employees, open and honest communication about company goals and performance, and a commitment to addressing and resolving employee concerns, such as 'We hold daily Team huddles to focus on well-being, tasks for the day, and any bottlenecks.'
- **Creating a Positive Work-Life Balance:** Creating a positive work-life balance can help reduce employee burnout and improve job satisfaction. This can include offering flexible work arrangements, and providing opportunities for remote work.
- **Employee Feedback and Engagement Programs:** Regular employee feedback and engagement programs can help identify areas for improvement, and provide a platform for employees to voice their concerns and suggestions. This can include regular one-on-one meetings, employee surveys, and focus groups.

Chasers Tip

- Develop a holistic approach that considers the needs and well-being of employees - even more so as we come out of the COVID pandemic, which has greatly increased mental health issues. By improving workplace culture, offering competitive compensation and benefits, providing professional development opportunities, improving communication and transparency, creating a positive work-life balance, and implementing employee feedback and engagement programs, small businesses can retain valuable employees and ensure their long-term success.

10. Lack of innovation - Failing to innovate can lead to a small business becoming outdated

In most cases, a business idea is intended to offer a solution to a problem; however not all of the ideas developed by entrepreneurs end up serving the purpose. It is what is called a solution looking for a problem when a product, service, app, or gadget developed or created because the entrepreneur thought it was clever runs the risk of not having an actual market problem that it solves. Sometimes a product or a service is just too early or too late to market. Getting caught up in the development of an idea often leaves the target market in a dilemma, and this is where customer feedback comes into play.

Every business entity tends to claim that the customer is king, but the case is usually altogether different. Only a small number adhere to this aim, and businesses that lose touch with their customers invariably fail – some fast, some more slowly. As the business owner, you need to keep an eye on the trending values of the customers. You have to find out if they still love the products or services that you originally offered, and what else they might like in the near future.

Your customers may like a product or service, but perhaps they would love and appreciate it even more if you changed this feature or altered that procedure. Are they in need of new features? What are they saying? Are you listening? What are the trends in the target market? Or is the market on the decline? As the business owner, ask yourself these and other questions. Maybe you are offering a product or service that has, well, fallen below trend.

Customer service and feedback are like manna from the gods. Your customers will tell you what they think if you listen to them and notice them. What are they saying on feedback forms, on social media? How many don't finish online transactions at the cart stage, and why? How many repeat customers do you have? What kind of referral system do you have in place? What are your Google Reviews saying about you? There's plenty of information and data readily available if you're interested enough to go looking.

No organisation should let its lifeblood spill. If the customers are being ignored, their questions unanswered, or are receiving mediocre customer service – they will share it. If no one is listening to their feedback or they get features or services they don't need or want, they will go elsewhere.

Then there is the need to understand all the factors surrounding the market, right from the product or service, the players in the same market and their products as well as the competition. Learn about the business's position in the market, and put all these factors and the externalities together as well. Furthermore, if all the capital is spent on product development and there is nothing left over for marketing, well, then the business has a big problem.

Another reason why so many Australian small businesses fail is because of mediocre sales skills. No matter which way you spin it, every business is selling something. Therefore sales skills are critical for all companies. All Team Members should have a clear understanding of what their business does, whom it helps and what its product or service achieves.

Businesses should never be static.

Businesses need to evolve with changes in legislation, consumer tastes and preferences, and, it goes without saying, technology!

Innovation is a critical aspect of any business, and unless you are looking inwards to see how you can do things differently, more efficiently, and to a higher standard, it's easy to become outdated and eventually fail. Here are several examples:

- **Lack of technology adaptation:** In today's fast-paced business world, technology is constantly evolving, and companies that fail to keep up risk becoming obsolete. For example, a small retailer that relies solely on physical storefronts and manual processes while competitors are transitioning to online sales and automation will struggle to remain relevant and competitive. COVID was a great teacher of this harsh lesson. Those businesses that adapted quickly to conditions - the early adopters - were able to attain greater sales and dominance in their market. Now it's generative AI.

- **Refusal to adapt to changing market needs:** The market is constantly changing, and companies that fail to recognise and respond to these changes can quickly become outdated. For example, in Warrnambool where I live, we have a diverse multicultural community, and if a small restaurant only serves traditional cuisine it may struggle to attract customers when there is a trend toward more diverse, international flavours.
- **Failure to adapt to customer feedback:** Customer feedback is crucial for companies to remain relevant and competitive, and those that ignore this feedback run the risk of becoming outdated. For example, an accommodation house that fails to respond to negative feedback posted on TripAdvisor may lose customers to competitors who listen and make changes.
- **Resistance to change:** In some cases, small businesses owners may be resistant to change, fearing it will disrupt established processes and routines. However, this may lead to a failure to innovate and finally render the business obsolete. Kodak and Blockbuster Videos are often cited as examples of companies that failed to innovate and, as a result, became passé and ultimately came to grief.

Kodak, once a leader in the photography industry, failed to keep pace with the digital revolution, and was slow to adopt digital photography technology. This led to a decline in its traditional film business, and the company was eventually overtaken by competitors who embraced digital technology like Apple and their iPhones.

Blockbuster Videos, once a dominant player in the video rental industry, also failed to adapt to changes in the market, including the rise of online streaming and digital downloads from newcomers like Netflix. The company's resistance to new technologies and changing customer demands finally led to its downfall.

Jenny Craig, the weight loss company founded in Australia, is a current example. A myriad of companies large and small as well as influencers have created thousands of apps and programs, and market them more efficiently. As a result, Jenny Craig Inc has failed after 40 years.

These examples spotlight the importance of innovation and the dangers of failing to adapt to changes in the market and technology. Companies that are slow to embrace new technologies and innovative business models risk becoming obsolete and losing ground to their competitors.

> **Our Solutions – Don't stop innovating or you risk becoming outdated and falling behind competitors**

4. THE CAUSES - WHAT ARE THE REASONS WHY BUSINESS FAIL?

Chasers
Tip
- Keep informed about industry trends, attend business conferences and seminars, stay open to new ideas, and implement them to continually improve the business
- Hire a business mentor or coach with their finger on the pulse of the changing business landscape
- Embrace new technology such as data analytics, AI, and all of the efficiencies and benefits these can bring.

11. Poor time management - Poor time management can lead to missed opportunities and a lack of productivity

Poor time management can have serious consequences for individuals and businesses alike. When time is not well managed, opportunities can be missed, productivity can suffer, and in the worst case, a business can fail.

One of the main ways in which poor time management can lead to missed opportunities is when someone fails to meet an important deadline. For example, if a business owner does not manage their time efficiently, they may waste an opportunity to submit a proposal for a new contract, causing them to lose business. Similarly, if an employee fails to manage their time productively, they may not complete an important project, which can lead to poor performance reviews and fewer job opportunities.

Another way that poor time management can lead to missed opportunities is in overlooking important details. For example, if a business owner is constantly multitasking, they may overlook important details, leading to mistakes. On the other hand, if an employee is not managing their time properly, they may overlook important details, leading to subpar results and missed opportunities for advancement.

In addition to missed opportunities, poor time management can also lead to a lack of productivity. This can happen because individuals are not able to prioritise tasks and complete the most important ones first. As a result, they may spend too much time on low-priority tasks, leaving little time for the high-priority ones.

Poor time management can evidently lead to business failure. If a business owner or employees cannot manage their time competently, they may not be able to meet the demands of customers and business, which can lead to customer dissatisfaction, lower profits and, in some cases, even bankruptcy.

Frank's Fast Freight

We all want the promise of FedEx when we need something delivered urgently - 'When it absolutely, positively has to be there overnight' - but Frank's Fast Freight did anything but...

They were not our customer, but we are using them as our example:

Frank's Fast Freight never stuck to their published business hours; the phone would ring unanswered, the gates would be locked at their business premises when they were supposed to be open, and of course the goods were never delivered when they should have been delivered fast. Now, if they had been able to deliver as promised, we would have made them our preferred freight service for legal documents requiring physical signatures, and so would other local businesses. We couldn't rely on them so chose a company we could trust.

Below par business practices resulted in missed opportunities, a lack of productivity, and ultimately business failure.

It is important to manage time productively in order to succeed.

Our Solutions - set clear priorities, create a schedule, and regularly review progress

In managing a business, it is important to create a plan for the year - both business and marketing - and then break this down into quarterly and possibly monthly plans.

Even three-to-five year plans help guide the business and its employees towards the vision to be achieved, as they provide context for decisions about different aspects of the business.

Setting out the goals for each quarter that relate to the 12-month annual plan in a 90-Day Action Plan helps build accountability and commitment.

> **Chasers Tip**
> - Assign each key person in your business a set of targets to achieve with the tasks they need to complete broken down so they can check them off to show their progress at daily or weekly Team meetings.

12. Lack of Systems & Processes

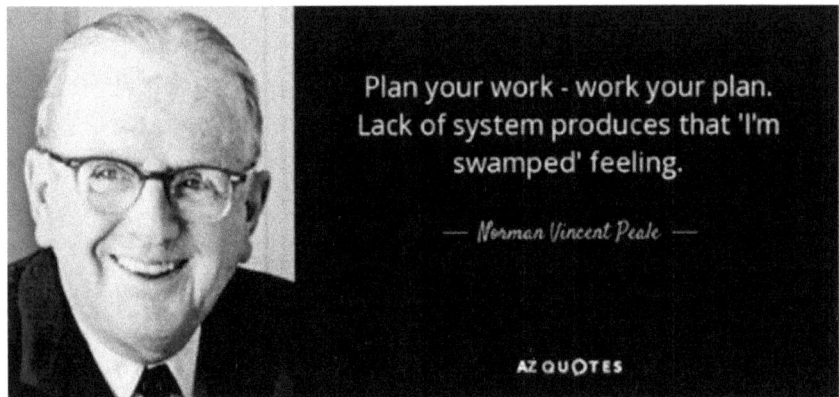

One of the key ways to free up your time in your business is to have someone else on your Team do the work.

However, most business owners will have all of the experience and knowledge 'trapped' in their heads and need to spend many hours teaching and training someone else to do what they do – or, at the very least, the simple repetitive tasks that are required day in and day out.

Without documented systems and processes, your business is limited in its ability to grow and scale.

A lack of systems and processes in a business can lead to failure for several reasons:

- **Inefficiency:** Without well-defined systems and processes, tasks can be repetitive, time-consuming, and prone to errors. This may result in a slow and inefficient operation that can negatively impact the bottom line.

- **Miscommunication:** Without clear processes in place, communication between employees, departments, and even with customers can break down. This can lead to confusion, misunderstandings, and mistakes, and the lack of quality control can harm the company's reputation.
- **Poor decision-making:** Without processes in place to gather, analyse and interpret data, decision-making may be based on incomplete or inaccurate information. This can lead to poor business decisions that may negatively impact the company's growth and success.
- **Lack of accountability:** Without systems and processes in place, it can be difficult to hold employees accountable for their actions. This can result in a lack of motivation, and a lack of commitment to meeting goals and objectives. And this applies to every role in the business, not just the Sales Team.
- **Increased risk:** Without well-defined systems and processes, a business is at a greater risk of security breaches, fraud, and legal issues.

Fiona's

Fiona's was another example of a small restaurant owner who was also the head chef. Fiona was responsible for managing the kitchen, organising the roster, ordering the ingredients, dealing with suppliers, creating menus, and handling the financials.

Her Team of six were doing their own thing with no consistency in method or quality. Fiona simply didn't have the time to create processes and train her Team Members, so they just did what they thought they should, based on what they knew.

Over time, Fiona became increasingly stressed, exhausted, and disillusioned as her restaurant wasn't going well. Customers didn't come back, and Team Members came and went, even though she was working long hours, advertising and marketing, and cooked great food. As a result, Fiona began to neglect important tasks such as recipe development and kitchen management, which resulted in less good food and poor customer service.

When she came to see us, it was too late. The reviews on Trip Advisor resulted in the restaurant having to close its doors, leaving her with nothing to show for her $400,000 investment.

Our Solutions - develop systems and processes, policies and procedures on all aspects of your business, from when you open up in the morning, HR and team rosters, handling customer complaints, and an organised inventory management system to closing the doors at night.

> **Chasers Tip**

Lack of systems and processes can lead to a wide range of problems that can irreparably damage a business's ability to succeed and grow. Implementing clear and productive systems and processes is essential for ensuring efficiency, accountability, and success.

At the other end of the spectrum is McDonald's: McDonald's is renowned worldwide for the consistency and quality of its food and service. You can walk into a McDonald's anywhere and know that you'll receive the same quality and service. What is perhaps not so well known is that the Australian McDonald's operation is a leader within the company in training and development of Team Members. It's so successful that it's not uncommon for 21-year-olds to be managing a $10 million a year franchise.

These are just some of the reasons why small businesses fail, and some possible solutions. It's important to remember that every business is unique, and that the best approach will depend on the individual circumstances.

13. Other factors that contribute to business failure

There's a myriad of reasons a business - your business - might fail, other than the ones I've outlined here. These include:

Unfriendly products or services

You might have a great idea but the product or service may be muddled and tarnished by bad user experience. If it is just too hard to use, it will not be used. If your website checkout doesn't work seamlessly, people will abandon their carts. If your customer service team doesn't help, your customers will leave.

Lack of focus

Without focus, you may be distracted from working in and on your business, and drop the ball too many times, resulting in customers leaving. If you don't care about your business and customers and put them first, they won't care about you. If you're not committed to delivering the best you can, you'll lose your competitive edge. And you need to keep your focus on your business continually over time.

Lack of capital and premature scaling

Insufficient resources can lead to an inability to bring investors on board IF you are looking for investors or a partner. Lack of money (current and future cash flow and retained earnings) within a business is an alarming sign. It indicates that they may not be able to pay their bills, loan, and other financial obligations. Capital problems make it difficult to grow a business, and may jeopardise daily operations.

Scaling is only a good thing if it is done at the right time. Scaling a business prematurely can ruin it as the expenses linked to scaling continue to grow at a rate not covered by the increase in customers. You can see this happening in the tech startup world, where phrases such as 'cash burn rate' and 'runway' and 'traction' have taken over from fundamental business principles.

- **Poor location** is a challenge that it may not be possible to overcome. If your business relies on the traffic of people in the city, location is a strategic necessity. It's also important to understand the wider environment of your location. What plans are there for new buildings, businesses, roadworks, traffic diversions? How secure is your landlord, and what is their reputation for dealing with issues relating to your premises? A poor location, or one that may be subject to far-reaching change, might make your customer acquisition cost too high, or you may lose customers altogether.

In one way or another, all of these factors have a hand in shutting down a business.

5
The Solutions - What Can Be Done to Reduce Business Failure?

Having looked at the various challenges, and how every one of them contributes to a business shut down, you should now have a better understanding of some of the causes and reasons why businesses fail, and be able to determine the best course of action for your business.

So what are the best practices and laid down framework for budding or existing business owners to prevent their business from failing, or at least minimise the damage? We've worked with over thousands of businesses, both struggling and successful, so we're in a great position to share learnings and insights.

Here are 15 ways to increase your chances of success in running your business:

- **Get professional advice** - Insurance against poor decisions that could set you back in time and money. Nowadays people assume that because there is so much information available over the Internet, they will find the answers to their problems. However in most cases, there is no substitute to sitting down with an expert who can show you how to connect the pieces you are getting all wrong, and the most suitable ways to fix things before it is too late.
- **Carry out market research** - It does not matter if you are selling a product or a service, you need to know the market demand. Who the other players are. It is crucial to determine if the market is well looked after - which in most cases it is. This means, as an entrepreneur, you will have to come up with better ways of adding value that give the customers reasons to deal with you, not the competitor. Offer differentiated products/services more conveniently - and it is vital to develop

other better ways to bring more people onto your doorstep by keeping up with market trends.

- **Prepare cash flow projections and budgets** to determine your costs, and the level of sales required to break even and make a profit.
- **Forecast and predict seasonal downturns** to know when you will have to inject some of your savings, or need a bank overdraft or short-term loan.
- **Prepare a business plan and a marketing plan.** It all begins with planning. The biggest mistake made by many entrepreneurs starting ventures is not sitting down and writing a Business Plan. Your Plan does not need to be a dense 50-page document. Any good, workable Plan fits onto a couple of pages. The goal is to keep it concise. An experienced business coach can offer assistance and guidance on writing a Business Plan.
- **Understand the timing of your tax obligations,** set up separate bank accounts, and allocate a portion of your tax collected from GST, employees PAYG tax, superannuation, and even income tax to them. In this way you will always have the funds available to meet your obligations. Profit First by Mikel Michalowicz is a book I would heartily recommend to anyone thinking about starting a business as it reinforces this idea of keeping money aside for specific purposes.
- **Prepare for the unexpected.** The COVID pandemic is a great example of being prepared for the unexpected. Many

businesses were forced to close their physical operations, some never to reopen, while others changed direction and saw opportunities to build a new business model with technology. Our office is a great example of this, as we foresaw business trends and had already invested in cloud-based technologies with our international Team Members back in 2018. As a result, we were easily able to move to online appointments booked with an online calendar link; data were uploaded to a secure cloud-based folder, and the finished tax returns and financial statements, etc., could be emailed and signed digitally.

- **The customer may be right, but must not be abusive or rude.** Most businesses were brought up with the notion of 'the customer is always right'. However, the stresses of living with COVID and running a business quickly saw this challenged as frontline Team Members bore the brunt of abuse for cancellations, delays, incorrect orders, and running out of stock. This took a heavy toll on many people and, as a consequence, saw Team Members take extended leave due to mental health issues and anxiety. This in turn created a domino effect as business owners could not cope with staff shortages - unable to replace staff, they could not work any more hours themselves. Great businesses value their Team Members and will not tolerate customer rudeness towards them. Sir Richard Branson has this brilliant take on this point with his quote *'Clients do not come first. Employees come first. If you take care of your employees, they will take care of your clients.'*

- **The right mindset - a positive mindset is required for business,** a mindset that combines hard work with having fun and smiling often. Hard work does not mean it has to be hard all the time though. You can take breaks with your Team, play games, sing karaoke, and celebrate birthdays and anniversaries. But you have to be committed. You have to give your business 110% almost all the time, show up ready to perform every day, lead by example, and have a great attitude.

A positive mindset is built from your self-esteem and a healthy self-image. If you have a keen sense of self-worth, you can put your entire being into action. A healthy sense of self-image and self-esteem can help you to trust your instincts -gut feeling - and take calculated risks, even when the going gets tough!

Many entrepreneurs believe they know what they're doing, but if they don't have a sharp focus on growing their business - a growth mindset - they may never learn. Without understanding your market - potential customers and competitors - you cannot plan, test or implement the right strategy.

If you lack confidence in yourself, your startup will likely fail. Andrew Constable from Forbes says that developing a growth mindset can prevent you from procrastinating. Like him, in my 40+ years of accounting and business, I have seen many business owners waste time procrastinating because they don't have a growth mindset. Instead of making a plan and taking action, they flounder and sit around thinking about what they should or shouldn't do - a major mistake that wastes a tremendous amount of time.

- **Accountability and responsibility of the owner:** Many businesses struggle because the owner treats them as a hobby. Right from the outset, you need to consider the business as a business. Think of yourself an employee, and pay yourself. Set measurable goals and hold yourself accountable, no matter what.

Running a business requires focus, commitment, and determination. Learn about the wide range of options, new ventures, and technologies. You cannot expect to get an ounce more out of your business than you put into it. Working on it for a short time means fewer operations and revenue - there are no shortcuts to success without hard work!

Owners can stay accountable in several ways:

Write down your vision and purpose for the business, record your goals and refer to them all the time. Keep them in front of you, and keep coming back to them - at least once a month.

Appoint an advisory board or get professional advice to help provide direction, and make the best decisions to take your business to the next level.

Join a peer advisory group or Mastermind that shares ideas and how best you can help one another boost the business systems. Find a coach or mentor who will point you in the right direction. The most suitable mentors and coaches are the ones with successful businesses themselves. Look for an investor, an angel or venture capitalist to solve your financial issues. Ideas will not move you; you need to take action to succeed. Wantrepreneurs are full of ideas that never result in action. Entrepreneurs are action takers (Zucchella & Magnani, 2016).

- All strong leaders and business owners need a vision

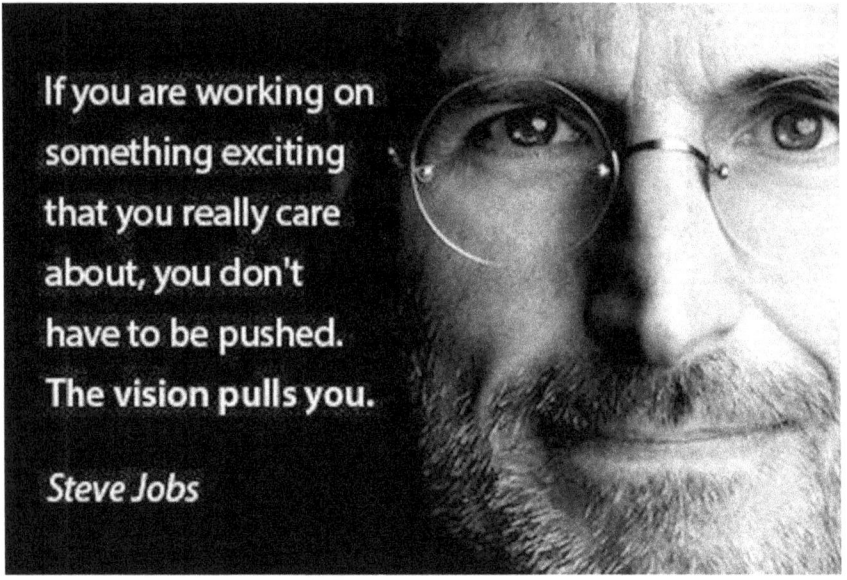

A vision is your picture of what the business looks, feels and sounds like, a mission - a plan - the road map to get there, and a purpose: the feeling that everyone, from the owner to the junior secretary, has when you accomplish what you set out to do. Purpose is when your values are driven by certain Team defined behaviors that create your culture. Having a

clear vision of where you want your business to head and a keen sense of purpose can guide you when things don't go as planned, and help you navigate those moments when you feel unsure of your next steps. Our vision and purpose was refined by my friend and mentor Paul Dunn.
Check Paul out on this podcast.

- **Take appropriate action as leaders** - Failure and dysfunctional leadership in business operations will always trickle down and affect every aspect of the process, from financial management to employee morale, and once productivity is hampered, failure looms large on the horizon. It is crucial for you as the business leader to learn, study, find a mentor, enrol in training, conduct personal research – do whatever you can to enhance and enrich your leadership skills and knowledge of the industry. Consider learning from and examining other best business practices, and see which ones you can apply.
- **Improve your product/service uniqueness and value proposition** - Implement measures that set your business apart from competitors. Ensure the conduct of your company is impeccable. Learn and understand your competitors' products

and services, and identify and know what they are better than you at.

Publicise your brand and set yourself apart. You will also need to step up your Marketing Plan and use as many venues as possible to present your brand to the public. You may be far better than your competitors, but that won't make any difference if your prospects do not even know you are in the game. Use social media, word of mouth, cold calling, direct mail, and other tried and true marketing techniques. Ensure you have a well-optimised online presence, develop lead generation strategies and contact information capture techniques such as offering first-rate content on your platforms and website, a subscriber newsletter, and information giveaways.

- **Build a solid business model** - Research and review the way other businesses operate in the industry. Develop a complete Business Plan that captures significant elements of the business operation, financial forecasting on predictable revenue, and strategic marketing, and challenge management solutions to overcome possible obstacles and competitor activities (Bridge, & O'Neill, 2017). Create a milestone chart with specific tasks, events, and objectives, and how they are all are measured along the way - and how to deal with possible challenges. A sound business model that incorporates best practices helps the business avoid failure, and provides a solid foundation.

- **Track what's measurable** - Business growth and development require much more careful and strategic planning than managing daily operations (Journal of Small Business Management, 2015). Even world renowned and profitable commercial franchises like fast-food restaurants and convenience stores conduct thorough research and planning before committing to a new location: measures on demographics, populations, existing competition, and trends, among other vital elements that seem defining in market decisions. Small business operators should do the same to avoid failure. Conduct sufficient research to make sure the time is right, and the funds for expansion are available. Provide stability in the first business before expanding to an additional location. Avoid purchasing unnecessary inventory that is unlikely to sell, but see to it that there is a plan in place to fulfill the demand should it arise. The key to successful growth and expansion and avoiding business failure is strategic planning.

- Good financial management

Use professional cloud-based business accounting software like our favourite Xero to keep track and records of all financial transactions, covering every expenditure and all revenues received, and use this information to generate profit and loss statements. Such information is vital, and essential to run a business. If you can, outsource this to an expert and meet them regularly for updates on how your business is tracking.

Stay profitable - this will address various challenges. Always keep an eye and your mind on profitability.

Manage cash. Entrepreneurs who fail often confuse cash flow with profit. The two are neither identical nor even similar. It is possible for you to go bankrupt with record cash flowing into your business. To succeed in business, a person does not just need cash flow: positive cash flow is what matters. Positive cash flow is when the cash coming into the business is more than the amount of money going out. It is simple, yet often overlooked. The companies that ignore this end up with negative cash flow, which is when the outflow of cash is more than the incoming cash. As a business person, you should never allow negative cash flow. Some of the practices you can use to improve cash flow include: partial payment in advance – ask for a deposit or full payment in advance. Only offer credit to customers selectively, but avoid that wherever possible. Focus on increasing sales. Offer incentives for early payment. Create a 'war-chest' or 'rainy day' account and arrange loans for emergency purposes.

Conclusion

Running a business is easy - no entrepreneur ever said!

Running a small business is hard - if it really was easy then everybody would be doing it!

It all starts with an idea and its conceptualisation. Identify the weak links, systemise and outsource or delegate where possible. Then work and improve on them. Disasters do occur, so always prepare for the worst. Have a contingency plan in place. Create systems of critical parts of the organisation, and build the business on them. Such systems are essential to recover from a disaster.

The failure of small businesses is a problem that we can and must address. People are not born knowing how to drive a car, yet millions have learnt. People are not born knowing how to drive business growth, but hundreds of entrepreneurs who have sought our advice or gone through our business coaching programs have learnt – and many more can learn if they are given that opportunity.

And this book is part of that education and solution.

Starting the Dream! - How to Avoid a Nightmare When You Start a Business provides a wealth of information and insights that are invaluable to anyone looking to start off. This book synthesises a comprehensive body of knowledge - my 40+ years of practical business experience as an accountant and business advisor - into a single, accessible volume, drawing upon the experiences of famous entrepreneurs, researchers, academics, and experts in the field. By identifying the most common reasons why businesses fail and providing practical strategies to mitigate these risks, the book equips readers with the tools they need to build a foundation for success.

Having read this book you should now:

- Realise that a clear understanding of the reasons and causes of business failure is critical before starting or buying one
- Be able to recognise the symptoms of business problems before they become contagious and/or terminal
- Be able to identify what should be done to reduce the prospects of business failure
- Be fully aware of the characteristics of successful businesses, which should ground you on the work required to not only survive but to also thrive.

Whether you're just starting out or are well on your way, **Starting the Dream!** - *How to Avoid a Nightmare When You Start a Business* is a must-read for anyone who wants to turn their entrepreneurial vision into reality.

The message is simple: with a thorough understanding of the challenges and a commitment to sound business practices, you can build a business that will endure for the years to come.

If you know someone who can benefit from reading this book,

please pass it on to them, and let's all help build better and more sustainable business communities together.

So, don't wait another day to avoid the nightmare and start the business of your dreams.

I hope that this book is an invaluable resource for you as you navigate the exciting world of entrepreneurship. Thanks for joining me on this journey, and I wish you all the best on your path to success in business.

10 Inspirational Quotes About Failure

1. Coco Chanel

   "Success is most often achieved by those who don't know that failure is inevitable."

2. Dale Carnegie

   "Develop success from failures. Discouragement and failure are two of the surest stepping stones to success."

3. Elbert Hubbard

   "The greatest mistake you can make in life is to be continually fearing you will make one."

4. Eloise Ristad

   "When we give ourselves permission to fail, we, at the same time, give ourselves permission to excel."

5. Henry Ford

   "One who fears failure limits his activities. Failure is only the opportunity to more intelligently begin again."

6. Michael Jordan

    "I've missed more than 9000 shots in my career. I've lost almost 300 games. Twenty-six times I've been trusted to take the game winning shot and missed. I've failed over and over and over again in my life. And that is why I succeed."

7. Ralph Waldo Emerson

    "The greatest glory in living lies not in never falling, but in rising every time we fall."

8. Robert Kennedy

    "Only those who dare to fail greatly can ever achieve greatly."

9. Thomas Edison

    "I have not failed. I've just found 10,000 ways that won't work."

10. Winston Churchill

    "Success is stumbling from failure to failure with no loss of enthusiasm."

Appendices

 1. The Ultimate Business Plan Template - scan QR Code to access

 2. 90-Day Action Plan Template - scan QR Code to access

 3. The Simplest Marketing Plan Template - scan QR Code to access

 4. 16-Point Business Legal Checklist to Protect Your Business & Minimise Risk

References

- (2015). Journal of Small Business Management, 53(1). doi:10.1111/jsbm.2015.53.issue-1
- Boling, R., Burns, M., & Dick, G. (2014). Social networking and small business: an exploratory study. Contemporary Readings in Law and Social Justice, 6(2), 122-129.
- Bridge, S., & O'Neill, K. (2017). Understanding enterprise: Entrepreneurship and small business. Macmillan International Higher Education.
- Burns, P. (2016). Entrepreneurship and small business. Palgrave Macmillan Limited.
- Burns, P., & Dewhurst, J. (Eds.). (2016). Small business and entrepreneurship. Macmillan International Higher Education.
- Colombo, M. G., Laursen, K., Magnusson, M., & Rossi Lamastra, C. (2012). Introduction: Small business and networked innovation: Organizational and managerial challenges. Journal of Small Business Management, 50(2), 181-190.
- DIISR&TE. (2012). Australian Small Business: Key Statistics and Analysis.

- Dwyer, B., & Kotey, B. (2015). Financing SME growth: The role of the National Stock Exchange of Australia and business advisors. Australian Accounting Review, 25(2), 114-123.
- Frost, H. (2019, June 22). Small businesses lament missed opportunities in SA Budget. Retrieved from https://www.abc.net.au/news/2019-06-22/small-businesses-sa-budget-impact/11236806
- Gerber, Michael (August 1995). The E-Myth Revisited - Why Most Small Businesses Don't Work and What To Do About It
- Gronum, S., Verreynne, M. L., & Kastelle, T. (2017). The role of networks in small and medium sized enterprise innovation and firm performance. Journal of Small Business Management, 50(2), 257-282.
- Haltiwanger, J., Jarmin, R. S., & Miranda, J. (2013). Who creates jobs? Small versus large versus young. Review of Economics and Statistics, 95(2), 347-361.
- Issue Information. (2015). Journal of Small Business Management, 53, 1-4. doi:10.1111/jsbm.12216
- Jones, N., Borgman, R., & Ulusoy, E. (2015). Impact of social media on small businesses. Journal of Small Business and Enterprise Development, 22(4), 611-632.
- Julien, P. A. (2018). The state of the art in small business and entrepreneurship. Routledge.
- Kotey, B. A. (2017). Flexible working arrangements and strategic positions in SMEs. Personnel Review, 46(2), 355-370.

- Kotey, B., & Sharma, B. (2016). Predictors of flexible working arrangement provision in small and medium enterprises (SMEs). The International Journal of Human Resource Management, 27(22), 2753-2770.
- Lignier, P., & Evans, C. (2012, August). The rise and rise of tax compliance costs for the small business sector in Australia. In Australian Tax Forum (Vol. 27, No. 3, pp. 615-672).
- Longenecker, J. G., Petty, J. W., Palich, L. E., & Hoy, F. (2013). Small business management. Nelson Education.
- Manning, A. (2015). How Data Can Benefit Your Small Business. Databases for Small Business, 1-15.doi:10.1007/978-1-4842-0277-7_1
- New study reveals why Australian SMEs fail - UniSA news releases. (2018, November 20). Retrieved from https://www.unisa.edu.au/Media-Centre/Releases/2018/new-study-reveals-why-australian-smes-fail/#.XSc4fv5S-M8
- Pupazzoni, R. (2018, October 30). Small business failures on the rise as retailers feel the pain. Retrieved from https://www.abc.net.au/news/2018-10-31/small-business-failures-on-the-rise/10447846
- Sampagnaro, G., Meles, A., & Verdoliva, V. (2015). Monitoring In Small Business Lending: How To Observe The Unobservable. Journal of Financial Research, 38(4), 495-510. doi:10.1111/jfir.12082
- Storey, D. J. (2016). Understanding the small business sector. Routledge.

- Westrenius, A., & Barnes, L. (2015). Managing complex business relationships: Small business and stakeholder salience. The Journal of Developing Areas, 49(6), 481-488.
- Zucchella, A., & Magnani, G. (2016). International entrepreneurship: theoretical foundations and practices. Springer.

Acknowledgements

The business world is a better place if we share our knowledge, experiences and ideas with others. What makes it even better are people who share the gift of their time to coach, mentor and encourage belief in future business leaders. Thank you to everyone who dreams of a better life and future for themselves and their families, their communities, their country and our world - and take the risk of acting on those dreams! The change you are making and have made is immeasurable.

The journey of life has taken me to a point where I feel compelled to help others understand the risks and challenges they may face in running a business - hence writing 'Starting the Dream'. To those business owners over the years that I have been privileged to be involved with, your insights, successes & failures, tears and laughter that we have shared together has allowed me to write this book to help others on the same path that you trailblazed before them.

To all the individuals I have had the opportunity to lead, be led by, or watch their leadership from afar, I want to say thank you for being the inspiration and foundation for the business we have created at Ceebeks Business Solutions for GOOD..

Without the experiences and support from my team, this book would not exist. You have given me the opportunity to lead a great group of individuals and build something of significance - a business that truly helps others achieve the dreams they are chasing.Thank you to Angie, Rocel, Janet, Shannae and Dale.

Having an idea and turning it into a book is as hard as it sounds. The experience is both internally challenging and rewarding. I especially want to thank the individuals that helped make this happen. Complete thanks to Jaqui Lane for guiding me in this process with her expertise on book publishing, my business colleagues Clea Jones, Angus Prior, Damien Patterson, Adrian Falk, Kimon Kalligas, Stacey Hughes, Cindy Mitchell, Ryan Goodwin and Debbie O'Connor for taking the time to read this book and provide your personal endorsements.

Finally, although they are the most important people in my life, a sincere thank you to my amazing Angela and daughters Dinah, Alli and Sofie for your endless love and support in anything I decide to take on and do.

About Ceebeks

Ceebeks Business Solutions for GOOD is a multi-award-winning accounting and financial services firm based in Warrnambool, Southwest Victoria, Australia. They are passionate supporters and champions of small business dedicated to helping them achieve the dreams they are chasing. They do this by offering a wide range of services including accounting, taxation, business coaching, mortgage broking and financial & estate planning.

Ceebeks' team of experienced professionals can help you with everything on the journey of life from starting a new business, sourcing finance, to managing your business, growing your profits and planning for retirement. They also offer a number of innovative tools and resources, such as their national award-winning digital magazine - the first online business magazine in Southwest Victoria, their daily blogs, weekly podcast - The Chasers Channel and business coaching program - Chasers Getting Results.

Whether you're just starting out, you're looking to take your business to the next level, or planning to wind down and retire, Ceebeks can help you achieve your goals.

Contact the Team on 03-55612643 or email shannae@ceebeks.com for more information about how their solutions can solve your financial and business challenges.

Links to Ceebeks Business Solutions social media channels & resources:

Website: www.ceebeks.com/
Facebook: www.facebook.com/ceebeks/
Instagram: www.instagram.com/ceebeks/
Mobimag: mobimag.co/chasing-the-dream
Spotify: open.spotify.com/show/3uWkwe55wtZrLErkDU3NoN

www.ingramcontent.com/pod-product-compliance
Lightning Source LLC
Chambersburg PA
CBHW062036290426
44109CB00026B/2641